# LET THE BIBLE BE ITSELF

## Learning to Read it Right

First published by O Books, 2008
O Books is an imprint of John Hunt Publishing Ltd., The Bothy, Deershot Lodge, Park Lane, Ropley,
Hants, SO24 0BE, UK
office1@o-books.net
www.o-books.net

| Distribution in: | South Africa |
| --- | --- |
| | Alternative Books |
| UK and Europe | altbook@peterhyde.co.za |
| Orca Book Services | Tel: 021 555 4027 Fax: 021 447 1430 |
| orders@orcabookservices.co.uk | |
| Tel: 01202 665432 Fax: 01202 666219 | Text copyright Ray Vincent 2008 |
| Int. code (44) | |
| | Design: Stuart Davies |
| USA and Canada | |
| NBN | ISBN: 978 1 84694 148 1 |
| custserv@nbnbooks.com | |
| Tel: 1 800 462 6420 Fax: 1 800 338 4550 | All rights reserved. Except for brief quotations |
| | in critical articles or reviews, no part of this |
| Australia and New Zealand | book may be reproduced in any manner without |
| Brumby Books | prior written permission from the publishers. |
| sales@brumbybooks.com.au | |
| Tel: 61 3 9761 5535 Fax: 61 3 9761 7095 | The rights of Ray Vincent as author have been |
| | asserted in accordance with the Copyright, |
| Far East (offices in Singapore, Thailand, | Designs and Patents Act 1988. |
| Hong Kong, Taiwan) | |
| Pansing Distribution Pte Ltd | |
| kemal@pansing.com | A CIP catalogue record for this book is available |
| Tel: 65 6319 9939 Fax: 65 6462 5761 | from the British Library. |

Printed by Chris Fowler International
www.chrisfowler.com

O Books operates a distinctive and ethical publishing philosophy in
all areas of its business, from its global network of authors to
production and worldwide distribution.
This book is produced on FSC certified stock, within ISO14001
standards. The printer plants sufficient trees each year through
the Woodland Trust to absorb the level of emitted carbon
in its production.

# LET THE
# BIBLE
# BE ITSELF

Learning to Read it Right

## Ray Vincent

BOOKS

Winchester, UK
Washington, USA

# CONTENTS

1. Great Expectations     1
   'The Maker's Instructions'?     3
   'The Good Book'?     7
   Food for the Soul?     11

2. What is the Bible Really Like?     17
   The Literature of the Underdog     17
   Works of Imagination     21
   Records of Passion     25
   The Result of Conflict     32

3. How did these Writings become "the Bible"?     39
   The Traditions of the Jews     39
   The New Way     43
   From Writings to Scriptures     48
   From Scriptures to Bible     53
   How Many Books?     56

4. Why These Books?     63
   Consolidating the Tradition     63
   Christian Scriptures: Sifting 'Heresy' from 'Orthodoxy'     64
   Which Jesus?     67
   Which Gospel?     69
   The Criteria     72
   The Books not Included     76
   Have we the Right Selection?     85
   Historical Accident?     89

5. Where is the Real Authority?     95
    Authority means Distortion     95
    Which Guiding Principle?     98
    The Church's Book, or Anybody's?     104
    The Bible or Culture?     109

6. Voices from another World?     117
    The 'Culture Gap'     119
    Let the Bible be itself     124
    Just a Drama?     128
    Our own Story     130
    The Ongoing Dialogue     134

7. The Bible and the Word of God     137
    Is Fundamentalism Evangelical?     137
    How does God Speak?     143

Suggestions for Further Reading     147

# PREFACE

This is not a scholarly book. In a very busy life as a minister I have made some attempt to keep up with the progress of academic studies, but I am not a scholar. I have checked the accuracy of the historical material in the book to the best of my ability, and I hope it will be a useful and reliable guide for people wanting to know more about how the Bible came into being. I hope too that it will be a helpful introduction for someone wanting to open a Bible and read it for the first time.

However, this is not meant to be a text book. It is an earnest plea for a more realistic, honest and truly Christian reading of the Bible. It dismays me to find firm Bible believers sticking to their own favorite texts and their traditional ways of interpreting them, while ignoring the vast treasures that are in the rest of the Bible. It dismays me just as much when "liberals" pick out the "nice" bits of the Bible and pretend it is really quite a liberal book. Both in their different ways impose their own beliefs on the Bible instead of listening to what it really says. I would rather honestly say "The Bible says this, but I don't agree", than say dishonestly, "The Bible seems to say *that*, but what it really means is *this*".

Fundamentalism of the very strict kind is a terrible danger in the world today. Most of us – whether Christians, Jews or Muslims – deplore the activities of those extremists who impose misery and violence on people in the name of Islam. We sometimes forget that there are Christian extremists who have similar attitudes, and that if the Bible were to be taken from cover to cover as God's authoritative law the result would be equal to the harshest Islamist regime. Without going to such extremes, there is already far too much use of the Bible as a weapon to encourage war, whip up fear and hatred, degrade women, restrict free speech, vilify other faiths and persecute homosexuals and other minorities.

It is sad too that many people, even sincere Christians, have reacted against this by assuming that the Bible – especially the Old Testament – is not really worth bothering with. The truth is that when we get away from the wrong kind of Bible-believing and start to discover the Bible as it is, we find a whole exciting and inspiring world opening up in front of us. I want to place on record my personal testimony that as a result of fifty years of preparing sermons, and of the study of which this book is one of the fruits, I love the Bible more than ever.

I hope this book will be helpful too to some people who come to the Bible virtually from scratch – who feel they would like to read it but don't quite know how to start. The Bible is not a collection of deeply wise spiritual sayings – though such sayings can be found in abundance in it. The Bible has a history and a function, which need to be understood if we are to get the best from it.

In referring to dates, I have decided to use the more modern expressions BCE (Before the Common Era) and CE (Common Era) rather than the traditional BC (Before Christ) and AD (Anno Domini). I am aware that the modern expression may be unfamiliar to some people and that some Christians may even see it as a denial of faith. However, in today's multi-cultural global village it seems more courteous for us Christians to refrain from constantly reminding the world that it was we who fixed the measurement of time!

Bible quotations (except where otherwise stated) are from the New Revised Standard Version.

I am grateful to John Henson, Professor Adrian Thatcher, Alec Gilmore and others who have offered very helpful comments, all of which I have taken seriously, and most of which I have accepted. The final version is of course my own responsibility.

# 1. GREAT EXPECTATIONS

Walk into any bookshop today and you will see a vast array of "Bibles" – "The Cookery Bible", "The Beauty Bible", "The Internet Bible", "The Diet Bible".... think of any branch of human activity and there will probably be a "Bible" for it. We understand "Bible" as meaning a book that tells you all you need to know about a subject in a clear, systematic way – a book that can be relied on for its accuracy and its comprehensive coverage. Find the "Bible" for your subject, look up the page that deals with your particular question, and you have the answer. Ironically, the Bible itself is not a "Bible" in that sense at all. It is not arranged systematically. It is not a concise guide to the teachings of the Christian faith, nor is it a straightforward book of rules for Christian behavior. If you want to know what Christians believe about God, or Jesus, or the ultimate future of the world, you had best get hold of a little book about Christian doctrine. To get the answer from the Bible you would have to search through the whole of it, and even then do a lot of the thinking yourself.

The Bible in fact says remarkably little directly about God. Its very first sentence tells us that God "created the heavens and the earth" But who is this God? To find the answer to this question you need to know where to look. There is no particular section of the Bible entitled "God: Nature and Attributes" where you can look it all up. Here are some of the statements made about God in different parts of the Bible:

"The LORD is merciful and gracious, slow to anger and abounding in steadfast love" (Ps.103:8)

"I the LORD your God am a jealous God, punishing children for the iniquity of parents, to the third and fourth generation of those who reject me" (Ex.20:5)

"It is a fearful thing to fall into the hands of the living God" (Heb.10:31)

"Our God is a consuming fire" (Heb.12:29)

"God is love" (1 John 4:16)

"Whoever has seen me (Jesus) has seen the Father" (John 14:9).

Most of what the Bible says about God is not in direct statements, but in stories of what God does. But this too can be confusing. The Bible tells us that God created the world and set the first man and woman in a beautiful garden. Yet in that garden he deliberately placed one tree whose fruit they were forbidden to eat. What its purpose was we are not told, but we are told that they disobeyed and were turned out of the garden, The Bible then goes on to tell us that after some generations God looked down on the wickedness of the human race and regretted that he had made them at all, so he resolved to destroy them with a flood. But there was one man, Noah, who was good, so God decided to spare him, his wife, his sons and his sons' wives. After this God regretted that he had destroyed the human race with a flood, and vowed never to do it again. Further on we read that God rescued the Hebrews from slavery in Egypt, visiting terrible plagues on the Egyptians in the process. He then led them into the Promised Land and instructed them to take over the land from those already living there and to slaughter them all without mercy. Throughout the Bible God delivers terrible slaughter on those who oppose him, yet Jesus says "love your enemies... so that you may be the children of your Father in heaven" (Matt.5:44-45).

Someone who wants to accept without question that everything the Bible says about God is true may well believe that there is some overarching truth that reconciles all these apparent contradictions. But even if this is the case it is obvious that the Bible, unlike all the other so-called "Bibles", very largely leaves us to work it out for ourselves.

## "The Maker's Instructions"?

This is just as true when we try to see the Bible as a book of ethical rules. Some people have called it the "Maker's instructions". God, they say, has made us, and in order to get the best out of this life, as with any product, we should follow the manual provided by the manufacturer. Certainly the Bible does contain a lot of "instructions", but when we start to look for them it is extremely confusing. The least user-friendly computer manual is crystal clear by comparison.

The first problem is where to find the rules. Like statements about God, they do not appear all in one section called "Rules for Living". They are rather chaotically interspersed with stories, genealogies, poetry, proverbs and sermons. You have to know where to look for them, and even then you find that some of them appear in more than one place and in different versions. Orthodox Jews do their best to follow the 613 commandments they find in the Bible, though they do not seem to advocate some of the punishments prescribed for breaking these command-ments. In fact, the kind of society created by the Islamist funda-mentalists most of us deplore could be equaled, if not surpassed, by anyone consistently putting into practice all the rules we find in the Bible. Christians who advocate the death penalty for murder on the basis that it is "biblical" seem not to have noticed that the Bible also lays down the death penalty for, among other things, adultery (Lev.20:10 etc.), homosexuality (Lev.20:13), worshipping other gods (Deut.17:2-5 etc.), and working on the Sabbath (Ex.35:2): this last instruction is backed up by an example of God decreeing the death penalty for a man who committed the sin of collecting firewood on the Sabbath (Num.15:32-36). According to the Bible, parents who have a rebellious son who eats and drinks too much have a duty to expose him to the elders of the town to be stoned to death (Deut.21:18-21).

We can only talk about the Bible as "the Maker's instructions" by applying to it an enormous amount of selectivity and/or self deceit. Even the most fundamentalist Christians do not in practice live by all the rules of the Bible. If challenged on some of the biblical dietary rules – the ban on eating pork and so on – they are quick to point out that these rules were part of the Jewish law that has been superseded by the Christian faith. However, they also mostly ignore the New Testament rule (Acts 15:29) that, whether Jewish or not, we should abstain from blood, which presumably means only eating kosher meat and not touching black pudding!

The problem is that when we use the Bible to establish rules, most of the time it is not rules we are quoting at all, but *examples*. An example is much more difficult to interpret than a rule. How do we know whether it is meant to be a good example, or an object lesson in what not to do, or perhaps something quite incidental that has no particular relevance for us as at all?

People today talk about getting back to "the biblical pattern of family life". But which pattern do they mean? The Bible tells us that Jacob, the ancestor of the nation of Israel, had twelve sons by four different women – his two wives and their maids (Gen.35:22-26). Then one of Jacob's sons, Judah, the ancestor of the Jews, and eventually of Jesus, only got any children at all because his daughter-in-law Tamar lured him by disguising herself as a prostitute (Gen.38). The Bible story seems to imply no condemnation of this, only admiration for her initiative! David, the great ideal king of Israel, had at least nineteen wives (1 Sam.18:27; 25:39.43; 2 Sam.3:2-5; 5:13-16), but the only time he was censured was when he stole another man's wife by plotting his death (2 Sam.11-12). David's son Solomon had seven hundred wives and three hundred concubines – even by today's standards that sounds like extreme promiscuity! Yet the only moral judgment the Bible story makes about it is that most of these women were foreign and drew him into the worship of other gods (1 Kgs.11:3-4).

Even the New Testament seems to have very little to say about the family. Polygamy is not specifically condemned – only of a bishop is it specifically said that he should be "the husband of one wife" (1 Tim.3:2)! Jesus apparently forbade divorce, but one version of what he says includes the words "except for adultery" (Matt.5:31-32; 19:9). In fact, most of the references to family life in the New Testament seem to be negative. Jesus and some of the other disciples (including Paul) appear to have been single, and even if they were not, Jesus seems to have encouraged them to leave their families and follow him. This "biblical pattern of family life" is very elusive.

What we say about the ethical "rules" or "patterns" of the Bible is just as true of the New Testament "pattern" of the Church. Christianity is divided into innumerable denominations who disagree about how the Church should be organized, while almost all of them claim to be following the New Testament pattern. Anglicans believe that the three orders of bishop, priest and deacon are sanctioned by scripture. Presbyterians find government by elders in scripture, while Baptists and Congregationalists find no hierarchy there at all but the autonomy of the gathered congregation. Baptists, on the authority of the New Testament, have no doubt that baptism means totally immersing someone in water when they voluntarily profess faith in Jesus Christ, but most other Christians are equally convinced that babies should be baptized with a small amount of water on their heads, and on the basis of their parents' faith. Pentecostals believe that the "gifts of the Holy Spirit", such as "speaking in tongues" are an essential part of Christian life, because this is how it was in the New Testament. Brethren follow the example of the New Testament in rejecting any idea of professional ordained clergy.

The fact is that the New Testament gives us few if any direct instructions as to how things should be done in the church. It is all a matter of inferring from examples. The New Testament *mentions* bishops, priests and deacons: does this mean that this is the divinely ordained order of the Church, or is it just that these are three of the different titles the early churches happened to use for their leaders? Accounts of baptism in the New Testament seem to imply that those baptized were adults who had made their own decision to become Christians – though even this is not entirely clear in view of the references to whole households being baptized (Acts 16:33; 1 Cor.1:16). And in any case, was this baptism of adults meant to be for all time, or was it just an inevitable feature of the first generation? Is "speaking in tongues" meant to be a normal part of Christian worship, or was it just a cultural feature belonging to that place and time, like foot-washing?

It is amazing how much people can deduce from a small amount of evidence if they are determined. There are at the most three references in the New Testament to the first day of the week being observed in a special way by the Christian community, we presume because it was the day of the resurrection. It was the day when they met together to "break bread" (Acts 20:7), and the day when a collection was taken for the relief of fellow-Christians in need (1 Cor.16:2). The book of Revelation (1:10) refers to "the Lord's Day", which we can presume means the first day of the week. The most we can confidently infer from these references is that Sunday was the day when the early Christians met for worship. Nowhere in the New Testament is it specifically stated that God has commanded Christians to rest on the first day of the week rather than the seventh day, much less that all the rules of the Jewish Sabbath now apply to Sunday! Yet this is what many generations of Christians, especially Protestants, have believed.

If we are to follow the examples the Bible gives in addition to the straightforward commandments, where do we draw the line? Jehovah's Witnesses, quite logically, refuse to celebrate birthdays, because only two birthdays are mentioned in the Bible: Pharaoh's birthday, when he hanged his chief baker (Gen.40:20-22), and Herod's birthday, when he beheaded John the Baptist (Matt.14:6-8). Therefore, they say, the Bible shows us that birthdays are only celebrated by wicked people, and no good comes of them. We could of course say, just as logically, that God does not approve of dogs because the Bible never says a good word about them, and in fact its very last chapter tells us there will be no dogs in heaven (Rev.21:15).

So we have a so-called "book of rules" that is complicated, ambiguous and very selectively observed even by those who profess to believe in it. This surely invites a naïve question: if God intended the Bible to be the "maker's instructions", why on earth did he not make them clearer?

### "The Good Book?"

When we look at what rules there are, not to mention the examples, we come against an even bigger problem. Would it be even morally right to obey some of the rules or follow some of the examples? A closer look at the Bible from an ethical point of view is bound to make us wonder how it ever came to be called "the Good Book".

If an armed force today were to invade a neighboring community and kill every man, woman and child in it, it would be universally condemned as a war crime. Yet this, according to the Bible (Deut.20:16) is exactly what God commanded the Israelites to do in Canaan. Later, we are told that King Saul fell out of favor because he had not obeyed God's command to kill not only all the Amalekites – men, women, children and babies – but also all their cattle, sheep, camels and donkeys (1 Sam.15).

There are of course passages in the Bible that present a vision of universal peace, beating swords into plowshares (Is.2:4; Mic.4:3), the wolf lying down with the lamb (Is.11:6-9; 65:25), and so on. Some Christians embrace complete pacifism on the basis of the teaching and example of Jesus. But most of the Bible, measured in terms of sheer column inches, glorifies war much more than peace, and a particularly brutal and uncompromising kind of war at that.

Of course, Christians usually interpret all this biblical

language of warfare as symbolic of the spiritual struggle of good against evil. Churches and school assembly halls ring cheerfully to the strains of "Fight the good fight", "Onward Christian soldiers", and "Stand up, stand up for Jesus" without an actual physical weapon in sight. The biblical images of warfare have become spiritualized. Or have they just been transmuted into religious militancy against those not of our faith? In today's turbulent world, where religion is a cause of bloody conflict in so many places, is it ethically responsible even to play with this idea that there must always be an enemy and a battle?

The first English settlers in North America, the Dutch in South Africa, and the Germans who first brought vineyards to Australia all saw themselves as somehow re-enacting the biblical story of the Israelites entering the Promised Land. They were God's faithful people seeking a refuge from oppression, and God was granting them this fruitful land. Because they were so sure of this, just like the Israelites, they had no qualms about robbing, enslaving or killing the people already living in the land. The British in the heyday of their empire saw themselves as God's chosen people, with a divine mission to occupy large parts of the world so that they could convert them to Christianity – a concept that in their minds also embraced "civilization" and trade. The idea of a chosen people may have become more and more spiritualized, but Christians are constantly reminded that they are "God's people", and encouraged to see themselves as having a special mission in the world – an idea that can still create the kind of self-righteousness and intolerance that is alien to the spirit of Jesus.

In the New Testament, too, racism rears its ugly head. In Titus 1:12 we find the saying "Cretans are always liars, vicious brutes, lazy gluttons" quoted with approval. One wonders how Christians in Crete cope with this stereotype inflicted on them by "the word of God" itself.

Even more dangerous is the anti-Semitism that finds its roots in the New Testament. In the first three Gospels, the enemies of Jesus are called "the scribes", "the Pharisees" or the "chief priests". In other words Jesus, like many other radical preachers before and after his time, fell foul of certain powerful groups in the community. This can happen whatever the nationality of the people involved. However, when we get to the Gospel of John we find a change in terminology. Here the enemies of Jesus are described simply as "the Jews". The fact that Jesus himself was a Jew seems to have been forgotten already – the Jews *as such* are now the enemy.

Already in the other Gospels the account of the trial of Jesus is slanted against the Jews. It casts Pontius Pilate, the Roman Governor, as a basically fair minded, if rather weak, man who had nothing against Jesus but was pushed into condemning him to death under pressure from the Jews. This bears little resemblance to the character of Pilate as portrayed by other contemporary Jewish writers, according to whom he was a brutal governor who showed no respect for Jewish sensibilities. Even the Gospels mention an incident in which Pilate mingled the blood of some Galileans with their sacrifices, which presumably means he slaughtered them at the altar in the Temple (Luke 13:1). Matthew's Gospel has him publicly washing his hands and saying "I am innocent of this man's blood; see to it yourselves", to which the Jewish crowd responds, "His blood be on us and on our children" (Matt.27:24-25) – words that have given Christians license to persecute Jews down through the ages, culminating in the horror of the Nazi Holocaust. Only in very recent times have Christian leaders repudiated the labeling of Jews as "Christ-killers", and even after the Holocaust the idea of the Jews as the enemies of Christianity dies hard. We cannot say of course that the writers of the New Testament had such murderous intentions. They were all (with perhaps one or two exceptions) Jews themselves. But the writings they produced, which became Christian scripture, already contained the toxic seeds of anti-

Semitism.

A further unavoidable fact about the Bible is that its culture is fundamentally patriarchal. Many Christians today still have a problem about accepting the equality of men and women, and if the Bible is their authority this is quite understandable. It is true that there are a number of examples in the Bible of women who broke out of the conventional role. It is also true that Jesus showed a respect for women that was unusual for his time and culture. However, no amount of selection and re-interpretation can get round the fact that the Bible comes to us from a world in which it was normally taken for granted that women were secondary to men. A woman was the property of her father until her marriage, when he handed her over to another man. In the New Testament we find Paul rejoicing in the unity created in Christ which means that "There is no longer Jew or Greek... slave or free...male and female" (Gal.3:28). Stirring rhetoric! But when it comes to the practicalities he very quickly back-pedals and refuses to allow women to preach or to exercise leadership in the Church (1 Cor.14:34-35).

In interpreting the Bible we habitually, often unconsciously, practice a kind of cultural translation. We say that some of the things the Bible says reflect the culture of their time, and if the biblical writers had lived in our time they would have put it differently. We talk of having to separate the "real" message of the Bible from the merely "cultural" features. But this leads to endless arguments as to which parts are culturally accidental and which are essential to the message. Into which category, for instance, should we put what the Bible says about the place of women in society and the Church, or about homosexuality, or about divorce?

On at least two moral issues Christians have long since turned their backs on what the Bible says. We all take it for granted that slavery is wrong, even though the Bible supports it as part of the normal order of society. On the other hand, our whole economy is based on the lending of money for profit, which the Bible for most of Christian history was interpreted as prohibiting. How can we honestly say that the Bible is our supreme moral authority? We would of course expect a book of absolute standards to challenge some of the attitudes and practices of present-day society. But what authority can it have when so many of its attitudes are alien even to a contemporary *Christian* conscience?

### Food for the Soul?

The marriage service in the Church of England, according to Common Worship, includes Colossians 3:12-17 among the recommended readings. This is a passage that talks about Christian love and patience – all quite appropriate for a marriage. But the recommended reading ends at verse 17, and it is in verse 18 that marriage is first mentioned! This part is obviously left out because sayings like "Wives, be subject to your husbands..." are offensive to modern sensibilities. But is it not rather peculiar, not to say dishonest, that we exalt the Bible as holy scripture while censoring out what it actually *says*? If what the Bible says about marriage is not altogether suitable, why not read from another book? But, we say, a Christian act of worship *must* include readings from the Bible. Somehow, what the Bible says is felt to be inherently more "holy" than what anyone else says, even if sometimes we have to censor it!

All the Christian churches make much use of the Bible in their corporate worship. In the Catholic tradition worship consists very largely of biblical psalms and canticles. Preachers of all denominations nearly always base their sermons on a "text" from the Bible. Most churches use a lectionary that prescribes Bible readings for every Sunday of the year. Lectionaries, however, are strangely selective, sometimes prescribing the omission even of half-verses because they might upset the congregation. People devising a liturgy for an unusual occasion often have to really scrape the bottom of the barrel for a "suitable" passage, and even then it has to be "doctored" a bit – all because no act of worship is felt to be complete without a Bible reading.

Not only in public worship, but in the personal life of believers too, the Bible has long held an important place. I remember when I was very young being challenged by a little booklet called *A Spiritual Check-up*. One of the questions it asked was something like this: "What do you most look forward to reading when you get up in the morning: (a) your mail? (b) the morning paper?, or (c) your Bible reading for the day?"

I had to admit that my order was (a), (b), (c), but I am sure the compilers of the questionnaire intended the reverse. How could a really spiritual person find any reading matter more exciting or important than the word of God? The logic seems unanswerable, but the fact is that even devout Christians usually read the Bible as a duty rather than a pleasure, and if they are honest they will have to admit that once they stray away from their favorite passages it becomes a rather tedious duty.

Many of us, particularly in the evangelical tradition, have been taught to say our prayers and read the Bible every day. The Bible is meant to be our spiritual nourishment. Of course there are many parts of the Bible that are a joy and an inspiration – good stories, beautiful poetry, comforting and uplifting thoughts. There are parts that are very relevant and challenging. There are even some parts that seem uncannily modern. But you have to know where to look for these passages, like oases in a vast desert of words. What do we really gain from reading the lists of strange names in Genesis and Chronicles? What is inspiring or spiritually helpful about the story of Abraham passing off his wife as his sister (Gen.12:10-20; Gen.20), or the tricks that Jacob and Laban got up to with each other (Gen.30-31)? What do we make of that strange little story about God trying to kill Moses when he had just told him to lead his people to freedom, and Moses' wife saving his life by cutting off her son's foreskin and touching Moses' feet with it (Ex.4:24-26)? How many Christians can remember offhand the content of such books as Obadiah, Nahum, Zephaniah, the Third Epistle of John, or Jude? How many have read them even once? How many believers are inspired by those interminable passages in the prophets that call down God's wrath on the Moabites, the Edomites, the Ammonites and various other "-ites" we have never heard of? How many of us are really interested in the theological arguments of some of the New Testament epistles, or the denunciations of heresies long since dead? The Bible is such a mixture of the relevant and the irrelevant, the exciting, the comforting and the tedious, that it demands a considerable effort to respond to every bit of it, from cover to cover, *in practice* as "the word of God".

Many Christians today no longer believe that the entire Bible is historically and scientifically accurate. They quite rightly point out that such a belief has to face the test of *facts*. But surely when people claim that the Bible speaks to us in some special, unique way as the word of God that too is a statement that has to face a test – the test of *experience*. Theologians use a lot of rhetoric about the Bible that does not bear too much examination. Do we really experience God addressing us in this special way every time we open the Bible? The honest answer given by most believers would be: yes, *sometimes*, in *parts* of the Bible. In that case, how can we justify talking in this wholesale way about the Bible as the word of God? How much of the material in the Bible is necessary in order for us to hear the gospel? How much of it is even compatible with the gospel? And if many parts of the Bible are neither necessary nor edifying, how can it be, *as a whole*, "the word of God"?

It is true that if we approach any part of the Bible in a spirit of prayerful expectancy we can feel that God is speaking to us in it. In my personal experience as a preacher I have often found this to be true. I have habitually either followed a lectionary or worked systematically through a book of the Bible. I have accepted the discipline of wrestling with all the difficulties of a passage –

trying to see it in relation to its setting in history, trying to hear what it said to its first readers, asking what it means in the light of the central Christian message, and so on. As a result of this I have often found myself getting quite excited about Bible passages that at first seemed very unpromising. And yet there remains a nagging question. Is this being quite honest? Does the fact that this can happen with any part of the Bible prove that the Bible is *uniquely* able to speak to us in this way? Most modern Christians in practice have drawn their comfort and inspiration from other books just as much as from the Bible, if not more. They have found it easier to hear God speaking to them in some of the spiritual classics, or in their favorite hymns. Those who follow a Bible reading scheme often find in practice that the accompanying notes are more helpful than the Bible passage itself.

In fact, if we were to approach almost *any* piece of writing with the kind of attention we pay to the Bible – dissecting it, analyzing it, reading it over and over, thinking about the meaning of its key words, and surrounding all this with a prayer for guidance – we would probably gain some significant insight even if the work itself was really not much good at all! How can we then say that the Bible – not just certain passages but the Bible in its entirety – is in some unique way the word of God? There seems to be too big a credibility gap between the rhetoric and the experience.

In so many ways the Bible fails to live up to the claims Christians have traditionally made about it. Its morality often falls far below Christian standards, its form does not lend itself to use as a book of rules, and it often fails to live up to the spiritual expectations people bring to it as "the word of God". But what if it was never really meant to be any of these things? Any book will disappoint or offend us if we misunderstand its nature. Try to read the telephone directory as if it was a novel and you will be bored to death before the end of the first page! Read a novel as if it was a history book and you could be seriously misled. In fact, some of the old Puritans condemned novels on the simple ground that they were untrue and lying is a sin! The way we read any book depends on our expectation, our idea of what kind of book it is supposed to be. Are the problems we find about the Bible the result of approaching it with the wrong expectations?

In order to have more realistic expectations about the Bible we need to understand something of what it really is: where it came from, why it was needed, what it was originally meant for, and how perceptions of it have changed in the course of history. But first let us try to forget some of the ways we have been taught to read the Bible, and take a cool look at it to see what kind of book it really is.

# 2. WHAT IS THE BIBLE REALLY LIKE?

The fact that the Bible has been traditionally regarded as an infallible authority, a book full of commandments from Almighty God, backed up by powerful people in Church and State, has conditioned us into thinking of it as a dominating, threatening book. We imagine the Bible writers as rather intolerant, censorious people who want to scare us into doing what they think is right.

Certainly there is an element of social control in parts of the Bible. Some of the commandments are obviously the work of legislators and were at some time in history part of the law by which early Israel or the later Jewish community was governed. Ezra, the man who seems to have been the founder of Judaism as a religious system, was obviously a stern Puritan, compelling people to strict obedience to God's Law. One of his acts was to command all the Jewish men who had married foreign women to divorce them and send them and their children away (Ezra 10). Parts of the New Testament, too, begin to display the desire for hierarchical order and obedience to rules that has characterized most of the history of the Christian Church. However, when we look closer, and especially when we look at the historical situation behind the writings, we find that much of what is said in the Bible comes not from the strong but from the weak.

## The Literature of the Underdog

The Hebrew scriptures were produced mostly at a time when the Jewish nation was under the thumb of foreign powers, or when individual Jews living in dispersion were suffering discrimination, mockery and sometimes physical violence. The real function of many of the stories was to boost the faith of downcast Jews and to reassure them that God was still on their side. While many parts of the Bible may seem bloodthirsty and vengeful to us, we have to look at them in this context.

The story of the Exodus from Egypt is central to the Jewish faith. It includes the ten horrible plagues inflicted on the Egyptians because Pharaoh would not let the slaves go, and then the miraculous crossing of the Red Sea by the escaping slaves while the Egyptian charioteers were all drowned. However, it has to be seen against the background of the little nation of Israel constantly living with the threats of its more powerful neighbor Egypt. There were times when this was not just past history – Israelites were still being enslaved, still being oppressed by Egypt or some other great empire.

The whole story of the Exodus conveys a message subversive of all imperial power. The pyramids the Egyptians built were symbolic of their society, as of many other societies: very broad at the base, and narrowing as they grew higher. At the top there was room for only one person, the divine Pharaoh. Applied "theologically", the logic of this was that there could not be many gods, but only one. This belief was actually proclaimed in Egypt round about the time of the Exodus. Some scholars think the Hebrews got the original idea of monotheism from the Egyptians. If this is the case there is a supreme irony in it, because the God the Hebrews believed in was one who identified himself with the slaves – not at the top of the pyramid but at the bottom.

The other stories of great acts of deliverance – the walls of Jericho collapsing at the sound of trumpets, Gideon defeating the Midianites with his three hundred men, the Assyrian army around Jerusalem disappearing overnight – were meat and drink to a people for whom defeat was a much more familiar experience than victory. The picture of young David killing the giant Goliath with one stone from his sling not only entertained many generations of children, as it still does, but it must have often seemed a message of hope for a little nation constantly surrounded by powerful heavily armed enemies. The stories of Daniel and his friends standing up to the Babylonian king were an encouragement to Jews to stand firm when their faith and their way of life were being threatened.

All this is the literature of the underdog. Unfortunately it has often been used, especially by the Christian Church, as a means of boosting the authority of the powerful and intimidating the weak into submission. The whole idea of divine judgment was originally meant as a reassurance to oppressed people that one day things would be put right, but it has too often become a way of threatening ordinary people with terrible punishment for their little personal "sins". Even today, right wing Christian politicians use the Bible in order to boost their power and justify war. This literature that grew out of the experience of the oppressed has often been taken over by the oppressors and become something quite different and dangerous.

One of the Bible passages modern Christians find most difficult is Psalm 137. Even the most reverent believer is tempted to call it "sub-Christian". It is the psalm that begins (in the version in the Book of Common Prayer with which many generations of Anglicans have been familiar): "By the waters of Babylon we sat down and wept: when we remembered thee, O Sion...". It is a lament of the Jewish exiles in Babylon, looking back to the tragic destruction of their city and their holy temple, and languishing in an alien land. But the "problem" is with its closing words: "O daughter of Babylon... blessed shall he be that taketh thy children: and throweth them against the stones."

This is by no means the most "unchristian" passage in the Bible – the instructions for cold-blooded genocide in the book of Deuteronomy probably win that prize. The reason why this passage is so often quoted as a "problem" is just that, being in the Psalms, it is more familiar and difficult to ignore.

This psalm is in fact a very moving piece of dramatic poetry.

If we were in the theatre and heard someone cursing their enemy and calling on God for revenge in this kind of language, we would not "tut-tut" or walk out in disgust! We would be caught up in the power of the drama, and go away saying what a good play it was. It is only the fact that the Bible has been set up as a theological and moral authority that makes this psalm a problem. If we view the Bible as a collection of the writings of human beings in a great range of situations, the psalm becomes a means by which we can enter into the tragedy experienced by that little kingdom of Judah more than 2500 years ago.

In fact, of all the Psalms this is one of the closest to our contemporary experience. If there had been television in those days, and we had been watching the destruction of Jerusalem as it happened, we would probably have had the same thought as the writer of the psalm. Things like that happen today, and our reaction is similar. Our first response to a terrorist outrage, or a massacre, or just the mugging of one innocent individual, is the feeling that those responsible should get a taste of their own medicine. We would like to see them punished, swiftly and painfully. It is only later, on reflection, that we realize this would not solve anything – that the answer is not blind revenge, but justice. Later still we may start to think about rehabilitating the wrongdoers, or even forgiving them. There is a powerful message of divine forgiveness in the Bible, but there are also passages like this one that express those feelings of vengeful anger that are a natural part of being human.

This psalm is a sharp reminder of the fact that much of the Bible is a cry of pain. It is the literature of people struggling to maintain, in spite of all the evidence, faith in a God who cares and will make things better. Even a popular and apparently innocuous Psalm like the twenty-third – "The Lord is my shepherd" – includes the verse "Thou preparest a table before me in the presence of mine enemies" (AV). The enemies are somehow always present: faith has to be maintained against the odds.

The same can be said of much of the New Testament. Jesus addressed his message to poor people, challenging them not only to trust in a heavenly Father who would meet their needs, but even to be generous with what little they had, believing that "the measure you give will be the measure you get back" (Luke 6:38). He promised that one day the poor would be rich, the hungry would be filled, and those who weep now would laugh while those who are laughing now would weep (Luke 6:20-26). He persuaded a motley group of Galilean fishermen and other ordinary people to follow him, promising that they would sit on thrones when he came into his kingdom (Matt.19:28). In a way the Christian faith, and the whole New Testament, could be seen as a way of coping with the fact that this kingdom did not come: instead, the one who preached it was executed, in disgrace both with his own people and with the imperial rulers. The resurrection was not a public event, turning the tables and showing everybody that Jesus was the Messiah after all. It was something the disciples somehow knew but could not prove, yet they persuaded many others to believe it. Christianity began as the faith of the defeated.

## Works of Imagination
It seems very irreverent to say that much of the Bible is the product of imagination. Even "liberal" Christians who recognize that the Bible stories are not necessarily accurate historical accounts feel uncomfortable about the idea that any of them could have been deliberately "made up". We like to talk in high-sounding theological language about the stories being essentially "true" in spite of not being factual. Scholars are very much at home when talking about "traditions" and the way they are adapted and shaped by their "transmission", edited and used by "redactors" and so on, but they are seldom willing to commit themselves to saying whether the events actually *happened*. However, if we can dare to take the step of saying that not only

were stories embellished in the telling (as all stories are), but that some of them were simply invented – that they never really happened at all – we can see the Bible in a whole new light. It then loses some of its false "authority" and comes alive as a truly marvelous work of the human spirit. And is not the human spirit after all a creation and reflection of the divine Spirit?

If we want to appreciate the imagination that created the Bible, we can start at the very beginning. There are two stories of the creation of the world. The first chapter of Genesis is a majestic poem describing how God created the heavens and the earth in six days by his powerful word alone. Then, in the second chapter, we find a simple homely story of a "hands-on" Creator molding a man from the mud of the earth and breathing the breath of life into him, then taking a rib from him and making a woman. Any attempt to "reconcile" these stories with a scientific account of the origins of the world, or indeed with each other, is not only misleading but an insult to the poetry of the stories. Here we have two very different, both beautiful, ways of simply *imagining* how God might have made the world.

There are many stories of miracles in the Bible: Sarah giving birth to a son when she was very old, Aaron changing his rod into a snake and back again to impress Pharaoh, the Israelites crossing the Red Sea on dry land, the sun stopping in the sky to give Joshua's soldiers a longer day to defeat their enemies, Elijah calling down fire from heaven on Mount Carmel, and so on. We can sometimes see stories that are an imitation of earlier ones. For example, the river Jordan drying up for the people to cross over into the Promised Land is a reflection of the people crossing the Red Sea as they came out of Egypt. We can see something of this too in the stories of Elisha, Elijah's somewhat less illustrious successor. Elijah, in a time of famine, asked a poor widow to give him some food. When she told him she only had a tiny amount of grain and oil left, he still asked her to share it with him, and from then on the grain and oil miraculously never ran out until the famine was over (1 Kgs.17:8-16). Of Elisha, it is said that a poor widow appealed to him for help. He told her to borrow all her neighbors' jars and pour into them the tiny amount of oil she had. She did this, and the oil was miraculously multiplied, so that she was able to sell it and pay off all her debts (2 Kgs.4:1-7). The widow who looked after Elijah had a son who died, and Elijah brought him back to life (1 Kgs.17:17-24). Of Elisha it is said that he received the hospitality of a rich woman who was married but childless. He prophesied that she would have a son, and the prophecy came true. This son died, and Elisha brought him back to life (2 Kgs.4:8-37). It is hard to avoid the impression that these stories about Elisha are imaginative revisions of the stories of Elijah, almost in the spirit of "anything you can do I can do better".

In the New Testament too we can sometimes see obvious little imaginative embellishments. In the story of the arrest of Jesus in Gethsemane, all four Gospels say that one of the disciples drew his sword and cut off the ear of the high priest's slave. Three of them say Jesus told that disciple to put his sword away, but only Luke says that he touched the slave's ear and it was healed (Luke 22:51). One can almost see Luke's mind working as he wrote the story and thought "surely Jesus would have healed the man". We can say the same of the statement that at the moment Jesus died the curtain of the inner sanctuary of the Temple was torn in two from top to bottom (Matt.27:51 etc.). If this actually happened it would have virtually proved his divinity. More likely, it was just one of those things one feels *ought* to have happened – a symbol of the cosmic significance of the death of Jesus. The whole story of the death and resurrection of Jesus in Matthew is much more spectacular than in the other Gospels – the dead coming out of their graves and walking about in Jerusalem at the moment Jesus died, the angel coming down on the morning of the resurrection and rolling the stone away, and so on (Matt.27:51-53; 28:2-4). If these things really happened, it is hard to see how the writers of the other Gospels could have been unaware of them. They look very much like imaginative embellishments of what Christian believers came to see as an event that changed the world for ever.

We are well aware that Christian imagination has embellished the biblical stories of the birth of Jesus. The "wise men" have become three kings. They have been given names – Caspar, Melchior and Balthasar – and one of them is often represented in paintings as an African. The inn keeper and the donkey, neither of whom are mentioned in the biblical story, are standard characters in Nativity plays, and at least one of the shepherds brings a lamb as a present for the baby. Some of these traditions go back a long way. There are tales about the birth and childhood of Jesus that go back as far as the second century.

This raises the question: what about the biblical narratives themselves? They appear only in Matthew and Luke: the rest of the New Testament has virtually nothing to say about the birth of Jesus. Moreover, the stories in Matthew and Luke are quite different from each other, and incompatible. The only things they have in common are that Jesus was born in Bethlehem and brought up in Nazareth, and that there was something miraculous about his birth. One cannot help feeling that these stories too are the product of imagination. It was common in the ancient world to attribute special circumstances to the birth of great men. There was also some pressure to explain how one who was known as "Jesus of Nazareth" could be the Messiah in view of the belief that the Messiah, being "the son of David", should have been born in Bethlehem. Matthew and Luke answer this question in two different ways. Matthew seems to assume that Bethlehem was Mary and Joseph's home, but that after fleeing to Egypt for a time they settled in Nazareth because Judea was no longer safe for them (Matt.2:23). Luke makes Nazareth their home, but says they had to go to Bethlehem for a census (Luke 2:1-4). There is no other historical evidence for this census, and surely even if it did happen it is inherently unlikely that the authorities would make everybody travel back to their ancestral home for it. These stories look like works of almost pure imagination, but who would want to be without them?

With many of the biblical stories, of course, we can assume that they are based on some actual event, but we can never be sure how much they have been exaggerated and adapted. We know from our own experience that every time we tell a good story it changes a bit. We adapt it to our audience, and we add little touches that make it a bit funnier or a bit more dramatic. Even if the story comes from our own firsthand experience rather than hearsay, we can rarely resist the temptation to say what we feel *ought* to have happened rather than the bare facts of what *did* happen. Many of the miracle stories in the Bible are probably exaggerated. To what extent we think they are exaggerated, or whether we think there is any historical truth in them at all, depends of course on our theology – how we understand "the supernatural", and whether and in what sense we regard Jesus as divine. However, whatever our views on these questions, it seems certain to anyone who is not a strict fundamentalist that imagination has played a large part in the making of the Bible. And again we may ask, why not?

## Records of Passion

The idea of the Bible as "authority" has led to our treating it as some kind of official legal document. We read it, whether in public worship or in private, to be informed of truth or to be given instructions. The Bible reading in church is often called the "lesson". This use of the word dates from a time when "lesson" was just another word for "reading", but most people now hear it in its modern sense with connotations of discipline and instruction: we sit still in our pews and listen to "Teacher" giving us the lesson. The person reading the "lesson" tries to do it with clarity and dignity. But reading the Bible in this way blinds us to one of its most important features, which is that large parts of it are the record of words spoken in *passion*.

The Hebrew prophets often seem pompous and rather paranoid to us, but we need to bear in mind who these prophets were and what were their concerns. For many of them, their function was to boost the morale of the people in difficult times. Their declarations of God's judgment on the nations around were often a kind of ritual designed to give the nation courage. Sometimes the words in themselves were thought to be powerful, like a blessing or a curse. When the prophet said the enemy would be defeated, and said it in a particular tone of voice, he was thought to be literally making it happen.

Some of the prophets, however, broke out of the mold and had a challenging message for the Israelites themselves. Their faith was firmly rooted in Yahweh, the God who had rescued the Hebrew slaves from Egypt and led them through the desert, the God who had chosen them to be a special people and made ethical demands on them, the God who was too powerful and mysterious to be represented by any image. They were dismayed and angry at the way the people had forgotten this unique God and fallen in with the agricultural gods their neighbors worshipped, with their idols and their looser ethical demands. They felt the urgency of calling the people of Israel back to being what Israel was meant to be.

As well as the drift into idolatry and polytheism, there was the change that had taken place as Israel was transformed from a confederation of tribes into a settled state ruled by a king and court. Some people were getting very rich. Others were getting poorer, becoming burdened with debt or even selling themselves into slavery – returning to the very state from which God had saved his people! The prophets saw this as a denial of Israel's original nature as a family. And so their preaching was concerned not only with the dilution of the worship of Yahweh but also with social injustice. The prophets were in many ways like the protesters and demonstrators we see today. Their verbal message was often accompanied by actions. Visual aids and street theatre (Jer.27:2; 28:10; Ezek.4, etc.) were all part of their repertoire. We can only do justice to these prophets by reading their words with the kind of passion in which they were first uttered.

One reason why it is so important for Christians to keep and read the Hebrew scriptures is that they help us to see Jesus against his background. He too was in the tradition of the prophets. He was not just a "teacher" in the now old-fashioned sense of someone standing in front of a docile audience and laying down rules. Nor was he a mystical guru teaching people to meditate and helping them to be calm and serene. He was, like the prophets before him, a preacher fired with a vision of what believing in God really ought to mean, and angered by the hypocrisy of those who were supposed to be the spiritual leaders. His passionate love for ordinary people and his anger at the way they were being treated made him lash out in provocative, shocking, often satirical preaching. Some of the religious leaders were understandably outraged at the way he knocked them off their pedestals and egged on the ordinary people to laugh at them. His upsetting of the money tables in the temple was a demonstration very much within the tradition of the old prophets.

The same is true of the much maligned Paul. Critics of Christianity (and some Christians too) see him as a dry, pedantic theologian who turned the message of Jesus into a complicated set of doctrines and imposed his own orthodoxy on everyone else. It is true that his line of argument sometimes seems abstruse to us, but this is because he was often addressing an audience that was steeped in the traditional rabbinical ways of thought. That aspect of his writing represents a culture that is strange to us, but would have been perfectly understandable at least to his Jewish readers. It is also true that in his letters he often comes out with very intolerant remarks. The most notable perhaps is in his letter to the Galatians: "But if even we or an angel from heaven should proclaim to you a gospel contrary to what we proclaimed to you, let that one be accursed!" (Gal. 1:8)

However, if we look more closely at Paul we can understand something of what he felt. Before he became a Christian missionary he had been the Christians' most feared persecutor. He had seen this new Jesus movement as a serious threat to the Pharisaic Judaism in which he was brought up and around which his whole life revolved. Then, in a dramatic experience on the road to Damascus, he was converted and became a Christian himself. The unusual way in which he became a believer gave him a way of looking at Jesus that was different.

First, he was overwhelmed with the sense of having been forgiven: by Jesus, by God, and (after some hesitation) by the Christian community. This last experience gave him a deep impression of what a transforming, community-building power had been let loose in the world by Jesus. There was a further dimension too: he had to come to terms with the meaning of the cross. Jesus had been condemned to death by the official leaders of the Jewish people. He had been condemned under the holy Law of God, and then hung up on a tree to die: something that, according to the scriptures, carried a special curse (Deut.21:22-23; Gal.3:13). If this Jesus was truly the Messiah, the Son of God, then that condemnation and curse in itself must have a new meaning. And so Paul came to his characteristic insight into the marvelous paradox of the ways of God: life through death, justification of sinners through the condemnation of God's own Son. To him, the crucifixion of Jesus had shown up the inability of the Law to sustain a real relationship with God, and so had brought about the end of its dominion and at the same time the fulfillment of what it was always meant to be about.

Paul's experience of the Christian movement had been mainly through the cosmopolitan community in Antioch, and he had seen for himself the joy and enthusiasm of people who were not Jews at all but had come to believe in Jesus the Savior and to embrace the new Christ-like life. He saw this too as part of what had been achieved through the cross. The whole human race was now seen to be on the same terms with God, deservedly condemned but freely forgiven. The distinction between Jew and Gentile was now no more, and Paul felt that he in particular had been called to be an instrument in bringing the Gentiles to faith in Christ.

The preaching of this message was the driving force of Paul's life. Is it any wonder, then, that he reacted angrily when he came across other preachers who contradicted it or watered it down? He saw would-be Christians from a Gentile background being put off by the moral censures and ritual strictness of some of the Jewish Christians, or being burdened with unnecessary guilt, and it made him angry. This Jewish-Christian fussiness and exclusiveness cut across his passionate enthusiasm for the new human fellowship he saw being created through Christ, where Jews and Gentiles could become one family. More than that, it denied in his eyes the fundamental principle that we are all offered free forgiveness through Christ simply by believing in him. To add any further demands was to nullify the good news.

With all this is mind we can easily see why Paul was so fiercely opposed to those who were diluting the message with rules and demands. Admittedly, there was probably something of the fanatic about him, and his relationship with the churches he founded had an authoritarian tendency. This was the nature of his personality. But at the same time it is possible to see that the principles he was fighting for were important, and to understand why he expressed himself as he did. He wrote in passion. It is only when people take his words as divine oracles and impose them as a rigid doctrinal requirement that this passion is corrupted into something it was never meant to be.

The passion that inspired many parts of the Bible can sometimes be frightening, as in the injunctions to ethnic cleansing in the book of Deuteronomy. These are rooted in the great vision of cosmic unity that was the raison d'être of the Jewish people, the conviction that there is one righteous God who creates and rules the entire universe, and that all idolatry is blasphemous and dangerous. The similar strictness of Ezra in "purifying" the race came out of the experience of the Exile, and the way in which Jews saw it as a judgment on the laxness and idolatry of earlier generations. We do not need to agree with these biblical passages, or to try to sanitize them and water down their meaning. We need have no hesitation in rejecting them, just as Jesus rejected the suggestion that he should burn down a Samaritan village that refused him hospitality (Luke 9:51-56). We only need to recognize that these things were said by those people in those circumstances, and to accept their existence as part of the complex journey of humanity in its search for the ways of God.

Anger is not the only passion in the Bible. There is a powerful stream of passionate love running through it. The often misused idea of the "chosen people" had about it not just national pride but an enormous sense of being blessed by a God who cared for a little, oppressed nation no matter how many enemies threatened them. At a time when the morale of the people was very low, a prophet hears God saying to his people (or to the prophet himself?), "Here is my servant, whom I uphold, my chosen, in whom my soul delights" (Is.42:1). These words are taken up in what is said to Jesus at his baptism, "You are my Son, the Beloved; with you I am well pleased" (Mark 1:11). The love of God is portrayed in the Bible not as a vague general benevolence but as something intimate and individual.

The very creation of the world was seen as an act of love. In the first chapter of Genesis we see God looking at everything he has made and finding it "very good". In the next chapter we see God molding a man out of the mud with his own hands, breathing into him the breath of life, then being concerned because the man is lonely, and so creating a fit companion for him. Love breathes through the whole story.

Sometimes we find God vacillating, torn between anger and mercy. This is a conception of God that cannot be fitted into the Greek-based philosophy of many Christian theologians. He is about to destroy the Israelites in his anger when they worship the golden calf, but he gives in to the pleading of Moses to spare them (Ex.32:30-35). He sends the prophet Jonah to Nineveh to warn the people that their city is about to be destroyed, but when they repent of their sins he repents of his intention (Jon.3:10).

This picture of a God torn by conflicting emotions reaches its supreme expression in the Book of Hosea, where the prophet learns through his own experience of an unfaithful wife something of the anguish of God, and how anger itself is part of love:

"How can I give you up, Ephraim...? My heart recoils within me; my compassion grows warm and tender. I will not execute my fierce anger..." (Hos.11:8-9). In the New Testament the theme reaches new depths: Jesus, who is one with God, crying out "My God, my God, why have you forsaken me?" (Matt.27:46; Mark 15:34) – God himself torn apart by love.

Even here, we need not feel obliged to accept certain doctrines because they are "in the Bible". Pushed to its logical conclusion, the traditional doctrine of "penal substitution", the idea that God demanded the death of his own Son before he could forgive the sins of humanity, and that he turned his back on Jesus because he could not look on sin, is morally unacceptable. Nevertheless, there are numerous references in the Bible to the death of Jesus as an atoning sacrifice, and it is surely possible for us to feel the drama of it and ponder it as a kind of poetic paradox without formulating a doctrine and imposing it as "orthodoxy". All this becomes possible when we stop looking at the Bible as an "authority" and allow ourselves simply to read it and to feel the passion that brought it into being.

## The Result of Conflict

It is very noticeable that the Bible repeats itself. Many of its stories appear more than once, in different forms. The history told in the books from Genesis to 2 Kings is told again in the books of Chronicles. Parts of the second Book of Kings are incorporated into the Book of Isaiah, so that, including Chronicles, they appear three times. (2 Kgs.18:13 – 20:19; 2 Chr.32; Is.36-39). Two of the Psalms (14 and 53) are virtually identical except that they use different names for God. The New Testament begins by telling the story of Jesus four times, with many minor differences and some quite major ones.

Among these repetitions there are often contradictions. Much of the Bible seems to be the product of an ongoing process of re-examining old ideas and producing new variations on them. If the Bible is supposed to be an absolute, consistent authority, the contradictions in it are a problem. But when we see the Bible for what it really is we can see that the contradictions are an essential part of its nature. Most of the writings of the Bible were born out of fierce controversy. Almost all those who contributed to it spoke in opposition to something. There was not a solid body of law or doctrine unanimously agreed and written down. The reality was an ongoing argument about what it was that God required. Many of the biblical themes go through a process of tension, development and sometimes radical transformation.

For example, the idea of the Israelites as God's chosen people is expressed in stories in which Yahweh is just a tribal deity leading his people into battle. But it is also expressed in the message of a prophet like Amos that God is only on their side when they act justly and rightly. It is expressed in Ezra's strict measures to purify the Jewish race and forbid inter-marriage with other nations, but it is questioned in the little book of Ruth that quietly points out that King David himself was the great-grandson of a mixed marriage. It reaches a climax in Isaiah 53, which seems to suggest that the "election" of the Jews is an election to suffering for the sake of the other nations. Then it is transformed in the New Testament into a gospel for the whole world, where Jews and Gentiles together become the children of Abraham through faith. So we find the first letter of Peter addressing a mixed collection of Gentiles and telling them they are "a chosen race, a royal priesthood, a holy nation, God's own people" (1 Pet.2:9).

The same kind of process happened with the theme of monarchy. This is usually represented as a divine institution founded on God's promise to David that his dynasty would be everlasting. The king leads the people in worship, and is God's representative. The temple in Jerusalem is essentially a royal sanctuary. Some of the Psalms show the king as playing a central part in the communal worship. This image of the king lies at the root of the whole concept of the Anointed One ("Messiah" in Hebrew) that became a focus of hope after the actual monarchy had fallen. Jesus was called "Messiah", or "Son of David". "Messiah" translated into Greek gives us "Christ", and so the very name of the "Christian" faith goes back to the Israelite concept of the sacred king.

And yet alongside all this there is the story of how Israel was originally a federation of tribes, "the children of Israel" with no fixed leader, and how (1 Sam.8) they angered God by wanting a king so that they could be "like other nations". Samuel pointed out to them at the time that this desire showed a lack of faith in the God who had always raised up a leader for them when they needed one. He warned them (in words probably put into his mouth by later generations from bitter experience) of some of the dire consequences of having a king. This anxiety is echoed in the insistence in the book of Deuteronomy that the king must not be like other monarchs whose word was law. He must have a copy of God's commandments constantly with him, and submit to them (Deut.17:14-20). There were evidently two quite different perceptions of kingship and its relation to faith in Israel's God.

To take a third example: large parts of the Hebrew scriptures are dominated by lengthy, detailed instructions for the rituals of the temple, which were largely a matter of slaughtering animals. The constant ritual shedding of blood was seen as the chosen means of communion between God and his people, and the way of atoning for their uncleanness and sin. This too came to have a powerful influence on Christian vocabulary. The language of sacrifice was often used in the New Testament to interpret the crucifixion of Jesus, and to this day Christians sing of being "washed in the blood of the Lamb". Yet in some parts of the Hebrew scriptures it is implied that this whole system of sacrifices was never demanded by God (Ps.50:7-15; Mic.6:6-8 etc.). It was an unnecessary distraction from a real relationship with him. His demand was not sacrifices but justice and mercy, a principle that Jesus himself quoted with approval (Matt.9:13; 12:7). The New Testament (notably the Letter to the Hebrews) develops the theme that animal sacrifices are no longer necessary because Jesus himself, the great High Priest, has made the supreme sacrifice for the sins of the whole world. On the other hand, the Gospel of Luke seems deliberately to avoid this kind of imagery when talking of the death of Jesus.

The very nature of God was the subject of intense discussion and often disagreement among the people who produced the Bible. The preaching of divine justice was a great incentive to believe that living a good life in accordance with God's commandments would bring safety and prosperity, and that disobeying them would bring disaster. This is spelt out over and over again in the Bible. A long section of the book of Deuteronomy is devoted to it. It lists all the blessings that will come if the people are obedient: good harvests, children, prosperity and victory. Then (at much greater length!) it lists all the disasters that will come if they are disobedient, summarizing it all with "I have set before you life and death, blessings and curses. Choose life..." (Deut.30:19).

The books of Judges, Samuel and Kings tell the whole history in terms of reward and punishment. When rulers and people are faithful and obedient to God, the nation prospers, but when they turn away from him the nation is defeated by its enemies. Then when they repent and cry out for help, he comes to their rescue and they prosper again. Of course, the history sometimes resisted attempts to force it into this pattern, and some explanation had to be found. For instance, Josiah was recognized as a good king, responsible for a great reform and purifying of the nation's worship. Yet it had to be admitted that he was killed in battle at the age of thirty-nine. The writer explains this as God's delayed judgment on the notorious sins of his grandfather Manasseh (2 Kgs.23:24-27).

This sense of suffering for the sins of the ancestors became intensified when the kingdom was destroyed and the people exiled to Babylon. Many people then looked back on the whole history as a working out of the statement in the Ten Commandments that the God of Israel is "a jealous God, punishing children for the iniquity of parents, to the third and fourth generation..." (Ex.20:5-6). Even after the Jews had returned from exile, we find Ezra confessing over again the sins of his ancestors, saying "you, our God, have punished us less than our iniquities deserved..." (Ezra 9:13).

However, an earlier prophet, preaching towards the end of the exile, had already expressed a different point of view: "Comfort, O comfort my people, says your God. Speak tenderly to Jerusalem, and cry to her that she has served her term, that her penalty is paid, that she has received from the LORD's hand double for all her sins..." (Is.40:1-2)

The prophet Ezekiel, around the time of the exile, tried to raise the spirits of the people by denying the whole concept of inherited guilt, saying that every individual is answerable to God for his or her own conduct: "it is only the person who sins that shall die" (Ezek.18:4 etc.). This kind of thinking helped to develop a more individual understanding of divine reward and punishment. The first Psalm makes the promise:

"Happy are those who do not follow the advice of the wicked, or take the path that sinners tread... In all that they do, they prosper. The wicked are not so, but are like chaff that the wind drives away..." (Ps.1:1-4)

In the centuries following the exile, when Jews no longer had freedom in their own country, and many of them lived in dispersion as a minority community, there was great comfort in this belief for those who strove to maintain their Jewish way of life in the face of mockery, poverty or persecution. However, it was not an easy faith to maintain in the face of reality. The good obviously do not always prosper, nor do the wicked always suffer. Psalm 37 is a lengthy consideration of this problem. Its answer, in brief, is "wait and see". The working out of God's judgment may take some time, but in the long run the righteous are better off and the wicked do not get away with it.

Even this answer, of course, is not fully satisfactory. The book of Job is a deep consideration of the whole question of divine justice. It tells the story of a good, upright man who suddenly loses everything: his property, his family and his health. In spite of the exhortations of his pious friends, who keep reminding him of the theology found in most other parts of the scriptures, he refuses to repent of his sins because he knows he has done nothing to deserve this kind of punishment. The book's conclusion seems to be that God does what he pleases and there is nothing we human beings can do to stop him: nevertheless we must worship him. In a sense the book ducks out of the problem in the end by saying that Job recovered from his sickness and enjoyed a long and happy old age. This, too, obviously does not always happen.

Eventually, not very long before the time of Jesus, when many young Jewish people were dying as martyrs, people began to see that, if God's justice is to be maintained, there must be judgment, reward and punishment beyond death. This belief is beautifully expressed in the Book of Wisdom (3:1-9; 5:15-16), but it was still controversial at the time of Jesus: the Sadducees did not accept it (see Mark 12:18-27). Also within the Hebrew scriptures was the book of Ecclesiastes, which questions whether there is really any meaning in life or history at all.

Divine forgiveness, too, raises problems. If God does not reward or punish, how can there be justice? But if God does not forgive, how can there be hope? The same passage in the Ten Commandments says that the God who punishes children for the sins of their parents "to the third and fourth generation of those who reject me" also shows steadfast love "to the thousandth generation of those who love me and keep my commandments" (Ex.20:6). Here there seems to be an idea of undeserved blessing that sits oddly with the emphasis of most of the biblical history.

The issue of divine forgiveness for serious wickedness is sharply raised in the book of Jonah. This little story tells how the prophet Jonah was sent to Nineveh, the capital of the huge, oppressive Assyrian empire, to warn its people of God's judgment. To his annoyance and dismay, the people actually repent, and God spares them. Jonah is incensed at this. He does not wish to live in a world where such wickedness is forgiven, but God remonstrates with him and leaves him with a question to ponder. This book does not quite go as far as the teaching of Jesus – "love your enemies" – but it at least raises the question of whether *God* loves them.

The Hebrew scriptures include a huge range of different points of view. Beliefs are questioned, argued about and sometimes completely transformed. With the birth of Christianity comes an even more radical transformation. Here the Jewish faith is picked up, shaken, turned inside out and let loose upon the whole world. But this was not the end of change and conflict. The new religion created its own tensions and became itself an ongoing argument.

And so the New Testament writings too were born in controversy. The Gospels were not just different creative ways of telling
the story of Jesus. The earliest of them, the Gospel of Mark,
already shows signs of trying to correct a previous image of Jesus.
Matthew and Luke evidently drew on Mark's Gospel for much of
their material. They repeat large passages of Mark practically
word for word, but often too they "correct" Mark in line with their
own point of view. Both of them in their original context were
probably intended to replace Mark, but some people thought
differently, so Mark continued to be used. This did not happen
with "Q", the document which probably lies behind other parts of
Matthew and Luke: assuming it once existed, it disappeared. In
Acts and the Letters too we find tensions among the early
disciples, who did not by any means all agree with Paul, and in
the Letter of James we find outright contradiction of Paul's
message of salvation through faith alone.

What we have in the Bible, then, is not a consistent, solid
corpus of truth but the written residue of a long, complex history
of many points of view, and sometimes sharp conflicts. If we insist
on regarding it as a set of infallible divine oracles calling only for
our reverence and obedience, we will miss seeing what a fascinating and lively collection of writings it really is.

# 3. HOW DID THESE WRITINGS BECOME "THE BIBLE"?

The Bible is, of course, not actually *a book* at all, but a collection of many books. The original Greek expression *ta biblia*, which was plural, meaning "the little books", or "the scrolls", has come into English as a singular word, "the Bible". We still talk about the different "books" in the Bible, but this too is a little misleading to modern ears, because most of them are much shorter than books in our usual sense of the word.

This huge collection of writings came into being over a very long period of time. The Hebrew scriptures, which Christians call the Old Testament, include primitive songs and sayings whose roots could go back thousands of years, and also the Book of Daniel, which comments on events in the second century before Christ. Even the New Testament writings, which were produced in a much shorter time, probably span a period of nearly a hundred years.

## The Traditions of the Jews

Most of the Bible originated in speech rather than writing. The people who produced it were not "authors" in the modern sense of the word, sitting down in their studies to write a book for publication. They were usually collecting and organizing material in order to use it for some specific purpose in the community – for liturgy, perhaps, or for teaching. Large parts of the Hebrew scriptures grew out of the worship, laws and customs of the people. Prayers and hymns, blessings and curses, words that were to be said on ceremonial occasions, were handed down as the older priests trained the younger ones. Stories and explanations were passed down through the generations as children were taught the history and customs of their community.

The books of the Prophets originated as live preaching. People stood up in the royal court, or the temple, or the market place, declaring what they believed God had inspired them to say. The expression "the word of God" originally referred to this powerful, immediate spoken word. If ever the words came to be written down, it was for a particular purpose. There is a story in the Book of Jeremiah (chapter 36) that illustrates this process. Jeremiah called upon Baruch, a professional scribe, to write down on a scroll all the things he had been saying over the years, and to go into the temple on a special day when crowds came in from the country and publicly read it so as to reinforce the message. Prophets often had circles of disciples who would remember their teaching, learn it by heart, and eventually write it down (perhaps after the prophet's death) in order to show how the prophet's predictions had been true.

The crisis that produced many of the writings we now have in the Hebrew scriptures, and the editing of those already written, was the conquest of Judah by Babylon in the sixth century BCE. By this time the nation of Israel had been reduced to the little kingdom centered in Jerusalem and called "Judah" because it was virtually just that one tribe. The "Hebrews" or "Israelites" were becoming "Jews" (i.e., people of Judah). This little kingdom had a proud past. Its king belonged to a dynasty that had been unbroken since the time of David, four hundred years earlier. The temple in Jerusalem was the spiritual heart of the nation, and considered to be the dwelling-place of God on earth. But the struggle to survive in the face of the powerful empires around eventually failed. Shortly after 600 BCE the Babylonians destroyed not only the city of Jerusalem and the Temple but also the community and its institutions by removing many of the leading citizens to Babylon.

Half a century later, when a new regime started encouraging

Jews to return to Jerusalem, the situation had radically changed. The Jews were no longer a nation in the territorial or political sense, but a community of faith. The main focus now was on preserving the commandments, the history, the collective memory of Israel as the "people of God". All the old stories, including the traditions of different tribes and regions, were gathered together and woven into one big story. It started with the creation of the world and went on to tell of how God had chosen Abraham as the vehicle through whom he would create a special people. It told how Abraham's descendants had been enslaved in Egypt, and how they had been miraculously brought out from there and led to the land of Canaan. On the way there God had given their leader Moses a set of laws by which they should live. Into this part of the story the compilers introduced a huge collection of laws both ancient and more recent. The story then went on to tell how the people had been persistently unfaithful and disobedient to their God, and how God had sent them prophets to teach them and warn them, and then eventually punished them by letting their kingdom be destroyed by the Babylonians. Through it all there was the sense of a purpose being worked out. God still cared for his people, and when they repented he was ready to forgive them and restore their fortunes. In addition to this "big story" there were the writings associated with the prophets, and other material such as psalms and poems, proverbs and philosophical reflections.

The history is told in the books from Genesis to 2 Kings. The two books of Chronicles were an alternative version written later, as were the books of Ezra and Nehemiah, continuing the story into the time after the exile. We cannot read these books as we would read a modern style history. They are a mixture of sober chronicles, legends and other material that is not narrative at all. Nor can we read them quite as we would read a novel. They do not come straight out of the mind of one creative writer. The people who formed them were collectors and editors. They used the materials they had to hand, writings and oral traditions that were already ancient. Some they adapted and altered, some they left more or less in the state in which they found them, and sometimes they wrote some material of their own to fill in the gaps.

Often these editors were anxious not to lose any writing that was ancient, and so they put together accounts that were not always consistent with each other. There are, for instance, two quite different stories of the creation of the world and humankind (Gen.1 and 2), and hints here and there of other versions, such as the idea of God measuring and laying the foundations of the earth (Job 38), or of defeating the primeval dragon of the deep (Ps.89:10; Isa.51:9). The account of Noah and the flood seems to be a weaving together of at least two stories, since the timing is confused, and while in some places it says that one pair of each species was taken into the ark in others it says seven pairs of "clean" animals and one pair of "unclean" animals. There is similar confusion in the stories about Abraham and those about the plagues in Egypt. And so what we have is not a clear, straight-forward story but a collection of writings of various kinds that can be confusing if we come to it with the wrong expectations. This is why many people who resolve to read the Bible "from cover to cover" give up before they have got very far.

Though the temple in Jerusalem was rebuilt and the priesthood restored, the emphasis of Jewish life after the exile had shifted. Many now lived in different countries and, though they went on pilgrimage to Jerusalem when they could, their religious life mainly revolved around their local synagogue, a meeting-place where they prayed and read the sacred writings. The focus of religion was now not so much on the sacrifices and the great public ceremonies (which could only take place in the Temple at Jerusalem) as on the remembering of the story. It was in this period that "Judaism" could be said to have started – a faith based on beliefs and stories enshrined in books.

One effect of the exile was the death of Hebrew as an everyday spoken language (the Hebrew spoken in Israel today is a modern revival and adaptation). The Jews were merged into the wider Aramaic-speaking community, and after the conquests of Alexander, around 300 BCE, Aramaic itself was overlaid by the spread of the Greek language throughout the Middle East. The knowledge of Hebrew was kept alive by the Jewish scribes and teachers as the language of religion. In the third century BCE, a translation of the Hebrew scriptures into Greek was begun in Alexandria for the use of the many dispersed Jews who were no longer familiar with the Hebrew language. At the same time the Jewish faith, with its belief in one God and its high moral code, was attracting the attention of many who were not of the Jewish race. One account of the history says that this Greek translation was actually commissioned by a non-Jew, King Ptolemy II, who wanted to add the Jewish scriptures to the vast library he was collecting in Alexandria. It was this Greek version, known as the Septuagint (LXX), that was "scripture" to most of the early Christians.

## The New Way

When the Christian movement began as a group within Judaism, scripture was a central element in the Jewish way of life. Rabbis taught the scriptures and argued among themselves about how to interpret them. Jesus himself would have been steeped in these writings from childhood, and as an adult he joined in this ongoing conversation. Many of his teachings as we have them in the Gospels are firmly based on the scriptures and his encounters with other rabbis, "scribes" or "teachers of the law" all revolve around the interpretation of scripture.

His early followers were just as closely bound to these scriptures. They proclaimed Jesus as the one in whom the scriptures were "fulfilled": that is, not just that certain predictions made by the prophets had turned out to be true, but that on a more fundamental level Jesus was the climax of the story of scripture. Matthew's Gospel has Jesus claiming that his purpose is not to "abolish" the law and the prophets but to "fulfill" them (Matt. 5:17). Paul, apparently quoting an already established formula among Christians, says that "Christ died for our sins" and "was raised on the third day" and both statements are followed by "in accordance with the scriptures" (1 Cor.15:3-4).

The early Christians not only quoted the scriptures in order to defend their belief in Jesus as the Messiah, but also constantly used the language of the scriptures in their worship and their thinking about Jesus. Many New Testament passages, without specifically referring to the Jewish scriptures, allude to them in ways that can only be spotted by someone familiar with them. We are always in danger of misunderstanding the New Testament if we forget how steeped Jesus and the early Christians were in what we now call the Old Testament.

At the same time, we need to remember that most of the early Christians knew the scriptures in the Greek translation rather than the original Hebrew. This translation in many places was different from the Hebrew. Sometimes a small difference in the translation of a word turned out to be significant. One notable example of this is Matthew's use of the prophecy about a virgin bearing a child (Matt.1:23, quoting Is.7:14). The Greek word means "virgin" in the literal sense, but the Hebrew word was more likely to mean just "a young woman".

Another example is in the Letter to the Hebrews (Heb.2:6-9) where the writer quotes Psalm 8. This Psalm is a meditation on the greatness of God's creation and the special favor given to human beings: "When I look at the heavens, the work of your fingers... what are human beings that you are mindful of them, mortals that you care for them? Yet you have made them a little lower than God, and crowned them with glory and honor..." (Ps.8:3-5). Here there are at least three instances of an alternative interpretation. First, the Hebrew (followed faithfully by the Greek and by the

English King James Version) literally says "what is man that thou art mindful of him, and the son of man that thou visitest him?". Secondly, the word here translated "God" is *elohim*, a plural form that could mean "gods". As such, it could also refer to God's heavenly retinue: the New International Version translates is as "heavenly beings" and offers "God" as an alternative. The Greek translation opted for the plural and rendered it as "angels". The King James Version followed this. Thirdly, the expression "a little" is rendered in the Greek by a word that means "briefly" or "for a little time". The writer of Hebrews was thus able to interpret the passage to say that God made Jesus (the Son of man) for a little while lower than the angels, and then crowned him with glory and honor.

Sometimes the differences between the Hebrew and the Greek were more substantial than this, probably because when the Greek translation was first made the Hebrew text was still not firmly fixed, and so we have inherited different versions. This explains why very often when the New Testament says "as it is written..." the words are quite different from those in the Old Testament as we know it. The New Testament writer is quoting the Greek, while the Old Testament we have in our Bible today is translated directly from the Hebrew Bible as handed down by the Jews.

The Christian scriptures - the New Testament - began in much the same way as the Hebrew scriptures, with the spoken word. Jesus never wrote a book, and, though there are books attributed to his immediate disciples (Matthew, Peter, John etc.) most modern scholars think it very unlikely that they were the actual authors. Jesus addressed his words to specific audiences in specific situations, often in response to questioning or "heckling" by his opponents. The things he said and did were remembered and repeated. Inevitably, they were remembered in different versions by people who saw and heard things in a different way. They were probably first written down in the note books of traveling preachers, and then gradually collected together into what we now know as the Gospels.

Before the Gospels were written, there were letters, and a large chunk of the New Testament as we now have it consists of letters written by Paul to various churches in the course of his missionary travels. There is very little of the formal "epistle" about most of these. They were mainly written for the same reason that people today write letters (or did, until the advent of the telephone and e-mail), that is, as a substitute for the spoken word when people are too far apart to talk to each other face to face. Paul, for example, writes to the Galatians: "My little children... I wish I were present with you now and could change my tone, for I am perplexed about you" (Gal.4:20). In writing to the Corinthians, he says at one point: "About the other things I will give instructions when I come" (1 Cor.11:34). If we ponder this statement it brings into question the whole traditional concept of the New Testament being the written blueprint for Christian faith and conduct. It clearly implies that we do not even know the bulk of Paul's instruction to the churches, because it was given by word of mouth. Nor do we necessarily have the most important features of his teaching: what we have is what he felt it urgent to say at particular times. His only reason for writing these things in a letter was that they could not wait until his next visit. If, when that particular question cropped up, Paul had been present in Corinth he would not have needed to write these things down, and we would not now be reading them in the Bible.

We have to remember, too, that even when things were written they were not originally intended as part of an authoritative Bible in the way in which we tend to think of it today. It is true that the writers of the biblical books, and the preachers and teachers behind them, thought of themselves as inspired to impart an authoritative message from God. Those who coined the commandments meant them to be obeyed. Some of them were probably legislators with the power to make laws that could be enforced, while others were idealists who believed that this was the way God wanted things to be done. The prophets often began their statements with "Thus says the Lord...", and those who wrote down their words to preserve them did so because they believed they were messages from God. Paul, as he wrote his letters to churches, was aware of himself as an apostle, that is, a man with a divine calling to preach God's message to the Gentiles. He wrote, therefore, from a position of authority.

This is true of most of the writers of the Bible. At the same time we have to remember that they were preaching or writing to a particular situation. They believed they had God's message to the people they were addressing at that moment, but they would not generally have thought of themselves as contributing to an authoritative book that would form the standard of truth for all generations to come. If they had known that religious communities thousands of years later would be treating their works as absolute authority, they would probably have written them more carefully!

In some of his writing, Paul is obviously being careful to distinguish between the teachings of Jesus and his own judgments. On the question of the sanctity of marriage, for instance, he says: "I give this command - not I but the Lord ..." However, a moment later, on the question of what a Christian should do if his or her spouse is an unbeliever, he says: "I say – I and not the Lord - ..." Later, on the question of virgins in the Church, he says: "I have no command of the Lord, but I give my opinion as one who by the Lord's mercy is trustworthy". He concludes this whole section by saying: "And I think that I too have the Spirit of God" (1 Cor.7 ). Paul here is certainly claiming some authority, but not claiming that his instructions are absolutely authoritative for all time.

The only book in the New Testament that apparently claims to be holy scripture is the Book of Revelation, which ends with the solemn warning against adding to or taking away from "the words of the book of this prophecy" (Rev.22:18-19). This echoes what is said in Deuteronomy about the commandments (Deut.4:2; 12:32). The fact that these words come at the end of the Bible in the form in which we now have it has often been used as an argument for biblical fundamentalism. It needs to be said, however, that the words clearly apply only to the Book of Revelation, and that of all the books in the New Testament this is the one least likely to have been intended for future generations – its whole message seems to be that the world is about to end. But this in fact is to some extent true of all the New Testament writers. They lived in the expectation of Christ returning in glory in their own lifetime. It would not have occurred to them that the world would still be here in two thousand years' time, and so the concept of being inspired to write a permanent book of doctrines and rules for the Church for centuries to come would not have been in their minds.

## From Writings to Scriptures

How did this miscellany of writings produced over a long period of time, and often originating in the spoken word, become "scripture"? There were several factors involved.

First, we have to recognize the mystique of the written word. Even the most educated of us today still sometimes have to shake off an instinctive tendency to assume that if we read something in a book it must be true. This assumption is especially likely to be made by people who do not read very much. We often find too that someone who has just read a fascinating book on a subject they knew nothing about before now feels able to talk about that subject as an expert! In the days before printing, the circulation of books was very limited. Reading and writing were the accomplishments of a very small minority of specialists: to the average man and woman, it was a mystery how anyone could draw knowledge and wisdom from a piece of parchment covered all over with strange marks. When just being able to read a book was an exceptional achievement, the person who had actually *written* the book was naturally thought to be omniscient, if not divine. The word "glamour" is thought to derive from "grammar" – both were seen as a kind of magic.

From very early times, books were associated with divinity. There are numerous references in the Bible to "God's book" in which are contained all the secrets of the world, human life and the future. Moses, when asking to die, says to God, "blot me out of the book that you have written" (Ex.32:32). One of the Psalms, reflecting on God's intimate knowledge of us, says, "In your book were written all the days that were formed for me, when none of them as yet existed" (Ps.139:16). The last judgment is expressed as the opening of books (Dan.7:10). In the Book of Revelation the secrets of the future are in a scroll that no-one but Christ can read (Rev.5:1-5), and in the New Jerusalem only those may live "who are written in the Lamb's book of life" (Rev.21:27).

With this kind of mystique attached to books and writing, it is not surprising that any writing, especially if it was religious, already had a head-start to become looked upon with reverence as "holy scripture". After all, the very word "scripture" comes from a Latin word that means simply "writing". Just the phrase "it is written" has an aura of authority about it.

Any writing of particular wisdom or beauty was thought in the ancient world to be "inspired". This idea is of course still with us today. We tend to think that any outstanding work of literature or art is not simply the result of efficient craftsmanship or persistent hard work, but of some extra, almost magical factor we call "inspiration". In the ancient world this was understood in a more literal way. A great creative artist was thought to be inspired by a god or a "muse". The Greeks did not read the epic poems of Homer simply in the respectful, appreciative way in which we may read Shakespeare. They believed this poetry was inspired by the gods, and so it followed that it must contain some message of importance from the gods to themselves. They looked upon Homer in a way very similar to that in which Jews and

Christians look upon scripture, including all the attempts to explain or allegorize the "difficult" bits that did not seem very edifying. This was characteristic of many ancient cultures, and so it is not surprising that in the Jewish faith, and then in the Christian faith, writings that had a specifically religious content, especially if they were in poetic form, would very easily come to be regarded as inspired, that is "breathed into", by God.

Another important factor in the ancient world was its great reverence for antiquity. There are places in the world today where the old are still truly respected, where people never try to flatter them by calling them "young at heart", or use silly phrases like "ninety years young", but simply call them "old man" or "old woman" as a genuine term of respect. In today's world, however, the frontiers of knowledge are constantly expanding. Each generation knows more than the last – parents trying to help children with their homework know this only too well! If we want to learn something today, we do not turn to the oldest book we can find, but to the latest. If we want to be really sure of our facts we may even mistrust the most recent book and consult a constantly updated web site. In a society like this, the old are naturally assumed to know less than the young, and as for those who lived centuries ago, we are surprised to find they knew anything at all!

The attitude of the ancient world was virtually opposite to this. Not only were older people assumed to be wiser because they had lived longer, but in some cultures people imagined that there had been an original "golden age" at the beginning of time, and that things had been gradually deteriorating ever since. This meant that the more ancient a thing was, the better it was. An ancient authority was always listened to with far greater respect than a mere contemporary. The Greeks in what we think of as their heyday, with all their remarkable achievements in art, literature and philosophy, still believed that no one could rival the wisdom of the ancient poet Homer. In the early centuries of Christianity we find that one of the arguments Christians used to defend their faith intellectually was that they had scriptures that were even older than Homer. Through most of the Middle Ages in Christendom scholars were more inclined to trust the ancient "authorities" than the evidence of their own senses. This way of thinking was yet another factor that inclined people to regard ancient writings as authoritative scripture.

Alongside all these, and perhaps the most important factor, was that the writings that came to make up the Bible were often designed for, and even more often used in, a context of worship. It is well known that the Psalms were to a great extent the "hymn book" of Israel. The commandments were probably read to the congregation gathered for worship at special festivals: there is an account of this kind of practice in the book of Nehemiah (chapter 9). Together with the commandments there was a lot of "sermon" material, exhortations to faithfulness and obedience such as we find in the book of Deuteronomy. Jews in dispersion gathered in synagogues and listened to the history of their people and the written words of the prophets.

This applies just as much to the early Christian communities. The letters of Paul were mostly addressed to churches rather than individuals, and so the natural way of communicating their contents would be for them to be read out when the church was gathered together, that is, during the time of worship. Letters were not only read publicly in the congregations, but also sometimes exchanged among different congregations. The letters of Paul were particularly valued, so that churches would naturally keep them and re-read them, People would make copies of them, either for wider circulation or because the original was wearing out. And so the letters of Paul, as well as other writings, would be passed down through the generations and reach a circle much wider than the churches to which they had originally been addressed. The fact that they were usually read in the context of worship, and regarded as giving authoritative guidance, meant inevitably that they came to be sacred texts.

Similarly, the stories and sayings of Jesus were most probably repeated when the early Christians gathered for worship, and as they came to be written down so it became customary to read them during worship. Justin, writing about 160 CE, specifically says that it was the custom of the Christians to meet together on Sunday and read "the memoirs of the apostles or the writings of the prophets".

There was already a strong element of authority in many of the writings that came to make up the Bible. The prophets prefaced their words with "Thus says the LORD". The commandments were given in the form of God speaking in the first person: "I am the LORD your God, who brought you out of the land of Egypt…" (Ex.20:2). In a society that worked by the exercise of personal authority, when democracy and "the hermeneutics of suspicion" had not yet been invented, it would be quite natural to yield without question to the authority of words framed like this. Similarly, Paul's letters were written in order to exercise his authority over the churches, an authority he believed he had received from God. The Gospels were obviously taken as authoritative from the beginning because they contained the teachings of Jesus.

By the time of Jesus most, but probably not all, of the books Christians call the Old Testament were regarded as holy scripture, and discussion about God and human duties revolved around scripture and its respected interpreters. Eventually the writings produced by the early church came, for Christians, to have scriptural status, but this took some time. The Second Letter of Peter refers to people twisting the meaning of Paul's letters "as they do the other scriptures" (2 Pet.3:16). This letter is generally thought to be the latest writing in the New Testament, dating from about the middle of the second century. There is also other evidence that this was the time when some of the Christian writings were coming to be regarded as scripture on the same level as the Jewish scriptures. Justin (c 160 CE), who referred to "the memoirs of the apostles" did not call them "scripture". A little later, Justin's pupil Tatian produced a harmony of the four Gospels (the Diatessaron) that enjoyed considerable popularity for several centuries. It is significant that not only did he "cut and paste" the Gospels to harmonize them, but he also omitted parts of them, and included other traditions that are not found in any of them. This suggests that the Gospels were not yet regarded as scripture in the sense of being sacred and unalterable. It was about the end of the second century that people began consistently to refer to the Gospels, the letters of Paul and possibly some other writings as "scripture".

## From Scriptures to Bible

The next step was for the "scriptures" to become "the Bible". The two expressions do not quite mean the same thing. We can realize this if we think of some of the other religious traditions in the world. Buddhism, for instance, has scriptures but no Bible. Buddhists recognize many books as "scripture", but do not set a clear boundary around a certain number of them, wrap them up in one book, and say "these, and these alone, are the scriptures". For Buddhists, the expression "scriptures" is a bit like the Western idea of "classics". In Western culture there are certain writings, and certain pieces of music, that are generally regarded as "the classics". Everybody has some idea which works belong to this category, but if we were challenged to make a list of them no two people would come up with the same list. Moreover, it is not only very old works that are regarded as classical: a new work can become a "classic" within a generation. For Buddhists and others this is the way things are with "scriptures". All holy books are revered, some more than others, but the list is not defined.

The religion that has the most clearly defined scripture is Islam. For Muslims, the Qur'an is a fixed entity, the word of God entirely revealed to one man, the prophet Mohammed. Even for Jews and Christians the situation is not quite like this. The Jewish scriptures consist of "the Law, the prophets and the writings". All are regarded as inspired, but the prophets and the writings are not quite on the same level as the Law, that is, the books of Genesis, Exodus, Leviticus, Numbers and Deuteronomy. This Law (Torah) is, for Jews, the supreme revelation of God: the rest of the scriptures are in some sense secondary. For Christians there are two Testaments. Both are scripture, but the New Testament is somehow primary. Many Christians would find it difficult to define exactly what the difference is, but it is real. Perhaps the most tangible expression of this is that in a Christian book shop it is possible to buy a "Bible" or a "New Testament", but if you go in and ask for "an Old Testament" you will get some strange looks! The New Testament is somehow able to stand on its own in a way the Old Testament is not.

Even after taking into account the difference between the Testaments, the Christian Bible is not such a simple thing as is often thought. On the most obvious physical level, we never see a "Bible" that is purely the words of scripture. In some Bibles we see short introductions to each book, headings to sections, some footnotes, and maybe a margin with cross-references. Most people realize that none of these things are part of the Bible itself – though people reading the lesson in church do sometimes read the section headings as if they were part of the text. However, not many people realize that this applies also to the titles of most the books. Most of the original manuscripts had no title. Perhaps even more surprising is the fact that the chapters and verses are comparatively modern. Chapter divisions came in gradually during the Middle Ages, but it was a Parisian scholar, Robert Estienne, around 1550 who first produced Bibles in which every chapter was divided into numbered verses.

The order of the books, too, is an historical development that is not part of the "original" scripture. For a long time there was no single volume Bible but a collection of scrolls. Different synagogues or churches would have stored them in different ways, just as we today all have our own individual method of arranging the books on our shelves. The whole idea of an "order" would have been meaningless. Christians from early times favored the "codex" form (that is, pages bound together between covers: the book as we now know it) rather than scrolls. This enabled a greater amount of writing to be bound up together, but it was probably not until about the fourth century CE that the whole Bible began to be produced in one volume. Even then the order of the books within it often varied considerably.

When we say that the Christian Old Testament is the Jewish Bible, this is not entirely true either, since the order of the books as we now have them is quite different. Both begin with Genesis, Exodus, Leviticus, Numbers, Deuteronomy, Joshua and Judges, but from there on they diverge. The Jewish Bible goes straight on to 1 & 2 Samuel, 1 & 2 Kings, Isaiah, Jeremiah, Ezekiel and then the Twelve Prophets (from Hosea to Malachi, in the same order as in the Christian Bible). Then, after Malachi, come the Psalms, Job, Proverbs, Ruth, Song of Solomon, Ecclesiastes, Lamentations, Esther, Daniel, Ezra, Nehemiah and finally 1 & 2 Chronicles.

This order may seem very strange to Christians familiar with their "Old Testament", but it is actually fairly simple. It is "the Law, the prophets, and the writings". The history books from Joshua to 2 Kings are regarded as part of "the prophets", but the two books of Chronicles, as well as Ezra and Nehemiah, are recognized as coming from a later time. Daniel too is seen as being in a different category from the prophets, a category known as "apocalyptic" (like the Book of Revelation in the New Testament).

The books from Genesis to Deuteronomy were consolidated relatively early as the Torah, or Law, and accorded supreme authority by the Jews. At the time of Jesus the expression "the law and the prophets" was the one most frequently used to describe the scriptures (see for instance Matt.5:17; 7:12). In just one instance in the New Testament we find the expression "the law of

Moses, the prophets and the psalms" (Luke 24:44). There is no evidence that at that time the Jewish scriptures were a "Bible" in the sense of a fixed, closed collection. Most of the writings we now have were regarded with great reverence and accepted as authoritative, but the Jewish canon, the official list of books that made up the scriptures, probably reached its final form some time in the second century CE. It then included the other miscellaneous books which the Jews called "the Writings".

The reason for the difference in order is that by the time Christians got round to deciding which books were holy scripture they had separated from the Jewish community, and so they made their own list independently. This list was based on the order: history, poetry, prophecy. Ruth was placed after Judges because it is a story set in the period of the Judges. The two books of Chronicles were placed after Kings because they cover the same history. Ezra and Nehemiah were placed next because they continued the history after the exile, then Esther because it was a story set in the Persian Empire, which succeeded the Babylonian. Christians placed Lamentations after Jeremiah because of the historical time in which they are set: in fact, there grew up a tradition that called the book The Lamentations of Jeremiah, though in the Hebrew there is no title. Similarly, Daniel was placed as a prophet following Ezekiel, because its stories are set in the period of the Babylonian exile.

The most striking difference is that in the Christian Old Testament the "writings" come in the middle and the prophets at the end. This fits with the Christian perception of the main purpose of the Jewish scriptures, to point to Jesus the Messiah. The prophets come last as a climax: it is as if Christian faith has re-shaped the Jewish scriptures into an arrow to point to Jesus.

### How Many Books?

If asked in a quiz, "How many books are there in the Bible?" most people would probably say "sixty-six". At least, this would be the answer from Protestants and those people in Europe, North America and other places who inherit a largely Protestant tradition. Roman Catholics and Orthodox would not be so sure of the answer.

At the time when Christianity began, scripture was not confined to the thirty-nine books of the Hebrew Bible as we now know it. There were numerous other writings that were regarded more or less as holy scripture. According to Matthew's Gospel, one of the sayings of Jesus strongly echoed a passage in Sirach (also known as Ecclesiasticus): "Draw near to me, you who are uneducated... Put your neck under my yoke, and let your souls receive instruction... See with your own eyes that I have labored but little and found for myself much serenity" (Sir.51:23-27; Matt.11:28-30). The little Epistle of Jude has at least two references to books little known by Christians today. It refers to a story in The Assumption of Moses about the archangel Michael disputing with the devil about Moses' body (Jude 9). Then it specifically mentions and quotes the prophet Enoch (Jude 14-15). This comes from the First Book of Enoch, an apocalyptic book written in the name of the ancient hero of faith who had "walked with God" (Gen.5:24; Heb.11:5). This book was particularly popular among Christians in the early days.

After the fall of Jerusalem in 70 CE the Pharisees, with their way of life that was not necessarily dependent on the Temple and could be practiced anywhere, were the part of the Jewish community that survived and shaped Jewish faith and practice from then on. The Christians meanwhile had withdrawn from Jerusalem and were becoming a predominantly Gentile group, and so before long there were two distinct religions, rabbinic Judaism and Christianity. Christians and Jews separately worked out which writings were truly part of holy scripture. The rabbis narrowed it down to thirty-nine books – the same books Protestants now call the Old Testament. The Christians, however, maintained a larger number, and never really reached a unanimous decision about which books belonged in their Old Testament.

The closing of the canon by the Jews was not without its influence on Christian scholars and theologians. Jerome, the great Bible translator who worked around 400 CE, judged that only those books that were in the Hebrew Bible were scripture in the full sense. The others, he said, should be read "for the edification of the people but not for establishing the authority of ecclesiastical doctrines". However, he included them in his translation of the Bible into Latin, which became the standard Bible of Catholicism right up to modern times (the Vulgate). His contemporary Augustine had no such reservations about regarding them as scripture. They were retained, interspersed among the other books of the Old Testament. The only difference was that, presumably because of the knowledge that they had been disputed, and were not part of the Jewish Bible, they were designated as "deutero-canonical", that is, the "second list". The situation is made even more complicated by the fact that some of the "deutero-canonical" writings are actually additions to fully canonical books such as Esther, Jeremiah and Daniel, so that not only some books, but some parts of books too, are "deutero-canonical".

At the time of the Reformation in the sixteenth century the question of the status of these writings was re-opened. Luther argued, like Jerome, that since the Old Testament is the record of God's revelation to the Jews we ought to respect the Jews' definition of its limits. A strong reason for his insistence on this was that certain passages in these books were being used to back up Roman Catholic beliefs of which he and the other Reformers disapproved: for example, prayers for the dead (2 Macc.12:43-45). It was therefore helpful to the Protestants' case to assert that these writings did not have scriptural authority. Luther, in his German translation of the Bible, gathered them together into a separate section headed: "Books which are not held to be equal to holy scripture, but are useful and good to read". The treating of these books as a separate unit labeled "the Apocrypha" is thus a Protestant invention. For Roman Catholics, "Apocrypha" has a different meaning (see below).

The Roman Catholic Council of Trent in 1546 came down firmly against Jerome and Luther, and confirmed that the Church accepted the deutero-canonical writings as being of equal status with the rest. Protestants, while disagreeing with this, continued to value them. The Thirty-nine Articles of the Church of England (devised in 1562) describe them as books that "the Church doth read for example of life and instruction of manners; but yet doth it not apply them to establish any doctrine" (Art.6). However, as time went on Protestants became less and less interested in the Apocrypha. Its omission from printed Bibles may well have been initially an economy measure: in the concern to make the Bible affordable to ordinary people, the Apocrypha was an optional extra they could do without. Later this omission became a theological principle: the Apocrypha was seen as part of the "heretical" Catholic Bible. In the twentieth century, as the heat of controversy cooled, more and more Protestant editions of the Bible appeared with the Apocrypha either between the Testaments or at the end. The Roman Catholic Church also entered into an agreement with Protestants that resulted in the Common Bible (1973), an edition of the Revised Standard Version that gathered the deutero-canonical books into a separate section between the Testaments.

Even the boundaries of the Apocrypha are not simple. Different Christian traditions have different lists. There is a kind of "penumbra" to the scriptures – books that are regarded as scriptural in some sense but not even qualifying as "deutero-canonical". For example, 3 and 4 Esdras and the Prayer of Manasseh are placed as an appendix to the Roman Catholic Bible and are called not "deutero-canonical" but "Apocrypha", while in the scriptures of the Greek and Russian churches they are indistinguishable from the other books. Of the four books of Maccabees, the first two are generally accepted as deutero-canonical, the third is recognized by the Greek and Russian churches, but not by the Roman Catholic Church, and the fourth only appears in an appendix to the Greek Bible. The Greek and Russian churches also have Psalm 151, which is not part of the Roman Catholic scriptures. The more one tries to grasp all these complexities, the more one realizes that the concept of "the Bible" is not a simple one at all. Roman Catholics are not actually able to say how many books are in the Bible because of differences in the way books are divided or welded together.

When we come to the New Testament, there is virtually unanimous agreement on the twenty-seven books, but this only came about after several centuries of uncertainty. It was not until at least the end of the fourth century that the exact extent of the New Testament was more or less universally agreed. This was a time when there was a particular concern about drawing the boundaries of holy scripture. Several factors contributed to this, but probably the main one was that from 313 onwards Christianity had become officially recognized by the Roman Empire, and there was political pressure for standardization. Constantine is known to have ordered fifty copies of the scriptures to be provided for use in churches in the city that was newly named after him, Constantinople. We do not know exactly which books were included in these copies, but this event (c 325-330) must have had considerable influence on the defining of the biblical canon. The earliest known list of the same twenty-seven books that are in our present New Testament appears in a letter from Athanasius, Bishop of Alexandria, written in 367. Several other individuals and church councils around that time made lists of the scriptures. There was still some variation, but increasingly the lists came to agree with one another.

The order of the books was even more variable. Manuscripts of the New Testament right up to at least the thirteenth century differ considerably in their order. Some put the Gospels at the end, some put John before Mark, some put Hebrews in the middle of Paul's letters, and some put Acts after the Epistles. One implication of this is that we need to be careful about interpreting texts in the light of their order, with arguments like "the Bible says this, but later it says this".

There has never been an official declaration of the exact extent of scripture by a body representing the whole Christian Church. The same list of twenty-seven books that we now know as the New Testament (though not in the same order) was given by the Councils of Hippo (393) and Carthage (397), but these councils were regional, not representative of the whole Church. The Roman Catholic Church made its first such declaration at the Council of Trent in 1546, but by that time of course Rome could not speak for the Eastern Orthodox churches nor for the Protestants. The Protestants in particular could not accept that council's canon of the Old Testament. In practice all Christian churches have the same New Testament, though even in this there is a slight variation. In Luther's translation Hebrews and James have been moved to a later position, just before Jude and Revelation, in line with Luther's contention that these four books were of less value than the others. In fact, in a Swedish Lutheran Bible produced as late as 1596 they were actually called "apocrypha". Moreover, to this day the Book of Revelation has never been included in the lectionary of the Greek Orthodox Church.

We have to recognize, therefore, that the Bible is not such a simple entity as many people think. There have always been arguments about its extent. Yet at the same time there has always been the *concept* of a defined, limited set of scriptures, a feeling that boundaries exist and are important, even though we may sometimes disagree about where they are. Unlike some of the oriental faiths, both Judaism and Christianity have felt the need for a "Bible" rather than an undefined collection of "scriptures".

We shall see something of the reason for this as we look more closely at the process by which it was decided which books constitute the Bible.

# 4. WHY THESE BOOKS?

## Consolidating the Tradition

When we read the books of Ezra and Nehemiah we can see that the Jews' return from their exile in Babylon was not quite the triumphal process that is sometimes pictured (see for example Isa.43:14-21). The reality was that some Jews, evidently with encouragement and help from the Persian king Cyrus, came from Babylon to settle and rebuild Jerusalem. As we know from later history, not all of them came: many remained in Babylon. Moreover, there was some tension between these settlers and those whose families had never left the land of Judah. In the time that had elapsed since the exile (at least fifty years before any of them came back at all, and probably longer for most) different communities had evolved with different traditions and attitudes. Nehemiah encountered opposition as he tried to re-build the walls of Jerusalem (Neh.2:19-20 etc.). There were disputes about who had the right to participate in the re-building and be part of the holy Jewish community (Ezra 4 etc.).

Ezra seems to have gained the upper hand, and there is an account (Neh.9-10) of his presiding at a public reading of the law of God and the people's solemn pledge to live in accordance with it. This event, of uncertain date but somewhere around 400 BCE, seems to have been the "launching", or confirmation, of the Torah as the basic law of the Jewish people, and in a sense the founding of Judaism as a religion. The "law" read out on that occasion was quite probably either the first five books of the Bible as we now know them, or something very similar. Certainly these books, before the rise of Christianity, had acquired supreme status as the foundation of the Jewish religion.

This was the core of the idea of a fixed, clearly defined body of holy scripture, though the exact definition of the Bible was not complete till much later. The chief motive in fixing the limits was to hold the community together in the face of the threat of dispersal and disunity. It was this consolidation around the Torah that enabled the Jews to survive when most of the other small nations the Babylonians had conquered simply disappeared from history. As time went on, this Torah came to be seen as an eternal sacred reality, the ultimate revelation of God. Judaism had become the religion of a Book.

At a later stage came "the prophets" and "the writings". The hardening process by which all these became the Hebrew Bible seems to have happened in that order: first the Torah, then the prophets, and finally the other writings. The process was probably completed in the second century CE, in similar circumstances to those that had prompted the fixing of the Torah. The rabbinic Jewish community needed to consolidate itself in view of the destruction of Jerusalem in 70 CE, followed by its complete abolition as a Jewish city in 135 CE, and in face of the competition from Christianity. The rejection of the books that Protestants now call the Apocrypha was probably due to a perception that Ezra had somehow wound up the whole business of divine revelation that Moses had started, so that only those books believed at the time to be no later than Ezra were included.

## Christian Scriptures: Sifting "Heresy" from "Orthodoxy"

A similar process of consolidation happened gradually with the writings produced by Christians. As the various movements inspired by Jesus, and the traditions that grew from them, were gradually consolidated into one Catholic Church, so the need was felt to standardize the scriptures. The formation of the "canon" of holy scripture was part of a general hardening and defining of authority. Most of the process took place in the second century, at a time when the Christian Church was becoming a fixed, settled institution with recognized leaders, defining itself against alternative versions of the faith, which it labeled as "heresies". The final stages took place in the late fourth century, when Christianity, under the patronage of the Roman Empire, was becoming an integral part of the social and political establishment. It was part of a general process by which Christian doctrine and the Christian order of society were being more firmly defined and established for the sake of stability.

And so part of the answer to the question of why Christianity has a fixed Bible is that, unlike some other religions, Christianity developed a stable, authoritative Church. There have of course been many divisions through the course of Christian history. In practical terms, it is more realistic to talk of "churches". However, the idea that there is *meant* to be one Church preaching one divine message has been present in Christianity from very early times, and the idea of a fixed, authoritative scripture naturally goes along with that.

At the same time, the very fact that the notion of a fixed Bible went along with that of a single Church means that the Bible, like the Church, developed very largely through controversy. The fixing of the New Testament came about through the controversies that raged in the Christian church of the first four centuries. The argument over different interpretations of the meaning of Jesus is already evident in the writings of the New Testament itself. In fact, Christianity came into being as part of the huge ferment of spiritual ideas that was characteristic of the changing, restless, cosmopolitan society of the time. Jesus was revered and interpreted in many ways and "hi-jacked" by all kinds of movements with varying religious ideas. The early Christian leaders and thinkers felt themselves to be defending the true gospel of Christ against a range of heresies.

Many of us today may be suspicious, or even scornful, of the notions of "orthodoxy" and "heresy", but this is partly self-deceit. We ourselves have a very strong sense that some things are true and others are seriously wrong. Often this is a "gut feeling". Many of us, when we encounter certain ideas – say, racist interpretations of Christianity, or the alignment of religious groups with extreme right-wing politics, or a sermon threatening "hell fire" for all who are not orthodox believers – will react by saying that this is not what *we* recognize as Christianity. The early defenders of orthodoxy were actually doing the same thing. Their views may have been different from ours, and the language in which they expressed them was different, but their motivation was similar. In the early centuries it was usually not a matter of a powerful universal church suppressing a minority whom it labeled as heretics. There were times when it was not at all clear which was the mainstream and which were the heresies. The views of the apostle Paul were quite probably in the minority during his lifetime – he was battling for his own personal vision of the significance of Christ. It was only later that his views came to be "orthodox" Christianity. The emergence of the mainstream Church was a gradual process. Some of the "orthodox" probably felt as if they were a despised minority in the face of widespread Gnosticism, Arianism and so on. It was only as the hierarchies established in Rome, Antioch and Alexandria came to a consensus that the picture emerged of a central "orthodoxy" dealing with a fringe of "heresies".

The "orthodoxy" of those early centuries was not something already settled. There was not, as there is for churches today, an already existing creed on the basis of which heresy could be condemned. Christians were still in the process of working out what they believed, and it was the controversies that moved that process on. Some people felt unhappy about the way others were expressing the Christian faith, and as they started thinking about why they felt unhappy their gut feelings became crystallized as doctrines. In a sense it was often the "heresy" that came first, and the "orthodoxy" that emerged in response to it. One could say that "orthodox" doctrines are not so much a statement of what the

Church stands for as a statement of what it *won't* stand for!

If we look closely at the so-called Apostles' Creed, for example, we can see how it was shaped by heresy. Pontius Pilate has the honor of being the only person mentioned in it by name other than the three persons of the Trinity and the Virgin Mary! This is not because of his virtue or importance, but because there were people at the time who denied the historical, earthly reality of Jesus. In view of this it was important to assert that this Jesus who is the eternal Son of God is also a real historical figure. The reference to Pontius Pilate pins him down to a certain short period in history, as a date would today.

On the other hand, in modern times much controversy among Christians has revolved around issues like the doctrine of the atonement, the inspiration and authority of scripture, the nature of the Eucharist, priesthood, church order and so on, none of which are even mentioned in the ancient Creeds. This is because, at the time when the Creeds were being developed, there was no controversy about these issues sufficiently serious to threaten the unity of the Church. And so the "orthodox" Christian faith that was worked out in those early centuries, including the canon of scripture, was largely a product of the perceived threats to it that were around at that time.

## Which Jesus?

One of these perceived threats was from a variety of sects and ideas generally summed up in the term "Gnosticism". This led Christian leaders to reject writings that suggested the Gnostic view of Jesus as some heavenly being, one among others. They wanted to insist that he was unique. The expression "only begotten Son of God" may be difficult to understand from a philosophical point of view, but it was meant to safeguard this principle.

Another characteristic of Gnostic sects was "docetism" – the idea that God had only *appeared* in Christ and put on some sort of show of death and resurrection. Those who became the main stream of Christianity insisted against this that Jesus was a real man of flesh and blood, who had really died on the cross and been raised up by God. The writer of the First Letter of John distinguishes true and false spirits by saying that a true spirit will confess "that Jesus Christ has come in the flesh" (1 John 4:2). The writer of Ephesians insists that the statement that Jesus ascended implies that he had first descended (Eph.4:9). It was important to establish that the divine Christ was the same person as Jesus of Nazareth, who had lived a real human life and really suffered and died. Salvation was not, as Gnostics thought, simply a matter of the education and enlightenment of the soul. It was reconciliation with God brought about through his Son dying on the cross. All the complicated arguments about the Holy Trinity which assumed such enormous importance in the fourth and fifth centuries were basically an attempt to express a conviction that was inexpressible and yet felt to be absolutely vital, that Jesus, the man, is God: not God in the appearance of a man, nor a man with divine characteristics, but fully God and fully a man.

When we look at some of the "gospels" that were not included in the New Testament, the most notable characteristic of many of them is the extreme exaggeration of the miraculous element. There are probably of course already some exaggerations in the stories we have in the New Testament Gospels, but these are nowhere near being on the same level as some of the fantastic stories in the other Gospels. The rejection of these as scripture was probably motivated by a feeling that the portrait of Jesus they presented detracted from the message by making it impossible to believe that such a person could really be human. Also, the portrait of Jesus as predominantly a mighty miracle worker detracted from the central theme of the gospel, that Jesus came to suffer and give his life for sinners.

## Which Gospel?

Another principle that guided the shaping of orthodox Christianity was the *openness and universality* of the message. Many of the Gnostic movements were rather exclusive sects or orders into which one had to be initiated. They preached a kind of spiritual caste system, that some souls are inherently superior to others and destined for different places in the heavenly hierarchy. Often there were secret teachings revealed only to those within the inner circle. Those in what became the main stream of Christianity firmly rejected any such idea. For them, the essence of the gospel was the good news of God's offer of salvation to all. We know from the New Testament itself that in the earliest days there was a great struggle to establish the principle that salvation was offered to the Gentiles as Gentiles, and not on condition that they became Jews. This, of course, was the great theme of Paul's ministry. Whatever resistance there was to it in the early days, it became an essential principle in the Church that Christ's death on the cross had broken down the wall that divided Jews from Gentiles and established one new humanity in Christ. It was largely in line with this principle that the canon of scripture came to consist only of books that were known and used by the whole church rather than just certain communities or regions.

Another principle that the mainstream Christian thinkers came to see as vital was that of *continuity with the Jewish tradition*. One of the most important factors in this sifting process was the stir surrounding the teachings of Marcion, a merchant who came to Rome in the middle of the second century and propagated his own distinctive version of the Christian gospel. Marcion was an over-enthusiastic devotee of the gospel as preached by Paul. For him, the good news of Christianity was that we are freely justified by God's grace in Christ, and that we grasp this by faith alone. In this he was no different from Luther and many other evangelicals down through the history of the church, but Marcion went further. His dogmatic obsession with salvation by grace alone led him to reject any expression that might call it into question.

First, he rejected the Jewish scriptures entirely. For him, there was no knowledge of the true God until Jesus came. The God of the Jews, with his legalistic commands, his wrath and his punishments, was a different being altogether. The true heavenly Father, who loves his creatures and forgives their sin, was revealed for the very first time in Jesus Christ. Christians, he thought, must forget about the Jewish scriptures and read only those writings that proclaim the grace of God in Christ.

But which writings were these? First, of course, the letters of Paul, who in Marcion's eyes was the true Apostle, the one who really understood the good news. Not even all the letters of Paul, Marcion thought, were genuinely his work. Enemies of the true gospel had adulterated them, and they must be restored to their original form. In this respect, though for different reasons, he anticipated some of the conclusions of modern scholarship about the letters of Paul. In turning to the Gospels, Marcion found them deeply infected with legalism and a doctrine of justification by works. He recognized only Luke as expressing the true gospel – and even Luke, like the letters of Paul, had to be carefully edited to get rid of what he considered to be later insertions and falsifications.

The impact of Marcion was one of the factors that stimulated Christians into thinking out their relationship with their Jewish heritage. By the middle of the second century most Christians were Gentiles, and Christianity was defining itself as a faith separate from Judaism. Marcion challenged Christians to think out the question: what is the status of the Jewish scriptures for Christians?

In spite of Marcion's attractive arguments, many Christians felt that their faith could never break away from its roots in the Jewish scriptures. The proclamation of the early disciples was that Jesus was the Messiah, the "Son of David" prophesied in the scriptures. They constantly drew on the scriptures not only to prove their point to fellow-Jews but also to deepen their own understanding of the significance of Jesus. It was a central plank of their message that Jesus had died for our sins and risen on the third day "in accordance with the scriptures" (1 Cor.15:3-4). Moreover, there was another practical reason for holding on to the Jewish heritage. Christian preachers were now engaging with the intellectuals of the Hellenistic world, and with the enormous respect for antiquity that characterized that culture it was a great advantage to be able to pin their authority to scriptures that were ancient.

In thinking this through, Christian theologians were drawn more and more to the concept of "covenant". In the Jewish scriptures God's relationship with his people is often described in terms of a covenant. In Jeremiah it is prophesied that God will one day make a "new covenant" (Jer.31:31), and Jesus himself at the last supper had called the wine "my blood of the covenant" (Matt.26:28 etc.). So the Christians of the second century argued that it was not, as Marcion claimed, a new God who was revealed in Christ, but a new covenant with the same God.

The Jewish scriptures thus came to be seen as the scriptures of the "old covenant", and Christian writings as the scriptures of the "new covenant". The Greek word was *diatheke*, which had been used in the Septuagint to translate the Hebrew *berith* (covenant) but which primarily meant a will. This made it a useful word for conveying the sense that this was not a covenant between equal parties, but rather an expression of the consistency of God's sovereign will – a firm promise made by God to his people. In the Jewish scriptures "covenant" was already associated with writing, as when it is said of Moses (Ex.24:7) that "he took the book of the covenant, and read it in the hearing of the people". This is probably an anachronism as applied to Moses, but the evidence of later times shows that the idea of a "book of the covenant" was current (see 2 Kgs.23:2; 1 Macc.1:57; etc.).

The perspective of Christians came to be that God, by the old covenant, had made Israel his own people, and by his new covenant had set down the terms of salvation for the whole of humanity. As these terms for the two sets of scripture came into general use (beginning in the late second century but not becoming common till the fourth), and especially as the Western Church used the Latin word *testamentum*, the meaning "covenant" tended to fade into the background, and the two "testaments" came to be thought of as the final declaration of God's will. This may have had some influence on the way in which Christians have thought of scripture ever since. "Covenant" suggests some kind of personal relationship, but "testament" has a colder, more official sound about it, encouraging people to read it like a legal document.

The challenge of Marcion not only stimulated the Church into full recognition of the Jewish scriptures as the "Old Testament", but probably also had its influence on the formation of the New Testament. The question had to be faced: is the gospel as preached by Paul the sum total of Christian faith? Was Paul, supported by Luke, so right in his understanding of Jesus that we have no need to read anyone else? The mainstream of orthodox Christianity thought otherwise.

### The Criteria

First, it asserted the validity of four accounts of Jesus. At some stage, probably around 200 CE, the Gospels of Matthew, Mark, Luke and John came to be recognized as constituting the standard, authoritative account of Jesus.

Marcion's exclusive adherence to one apostle possibly also influenced the church in accepting some of the other letters we now have in the New Testament – those of James, Peter, John and Jude. These writings seem to have been much slower in finding acceptance than those of Paul. This is probably because Paul's letters were gathered into a collection at a fairly early stage and widely known in Asia Minor, Greece and Rome, while these other letters were known only in certain regions. It could also be because, as most modern scholars think, few if any of these letters are genuinely the work of the apostles after whom they were named. They are more likely to have been produced by communities with some kind of tradition going back to those apostles. Eventually, however, these letters also came to be accepted as part of Christian scripture, and part of the motive for this may have been a desire to make the point that the teaching of the Church was based on all the apostles, not just Paul.

Another challenge in the second century came from Montanism. This was a charismatic movement that emerged in Phrygia, led by Montanus and his two female companions, Prisca and Maximilla. It proclaimed a new outpouring of the Holy Spirit and the imminent coming of the New Jerusalem. There was a great emphasis on prophecy and new revelation through the Holy Spirit, which tended to detract from the authority of scripture and the historical Christian tradition. In the face of this phenomenon, it had to be asserted that God is revealed not just through the inspiration of the moment, but through the actual teaching of Jesus of Nazareth and his early disciples. However much we may be inspired by the Spirit, the Christian faith must be rooted in a particular history and the writings that witness to that history.

And so, particularly in the second century, the crucial question was: who has the authentic tradition, i.e., the message of Christ as it has been from the beginning? In order to establish this, the Church had to hold on to those documents that everyone agreed were primary – the documents that were believed to be written, directly or indirectly, by an apostle, and had been consistently used throughout the Church from the beginning. We have to say "directly or indirectly" because even when we think of the four accepted Gospels, two were quite clearly not the work of an apostle. However, there was a tradition that attributed Mark's

Gospel to John Mark, who was close to Peter and taught by him. Luke was known to be a close associate of Paul (Col.4:14; 2 Tim.4:11; Phile.24), and some passages in the Acts of the Apostles (21:1,5,6; etc.) imply that he traveled with him. And so the Gospels of Mark and Luke were closely tied to the authority of the two supreme apostles, Peter and Paul.

Outside the Gospels and Acts, most of the New Testament consists of letters written by Paul or attributed to him. Paul, of course, was not one of the original Twelve. However, he had always claimed to be an apostle (a special messenger) called directly by God to take the gospel to the Gentiles. In fact, he was considered by many to be *"the* Apostle". The term could even have been originally coined by him and later applied to the twelve chosen by Jesus.

Alongside the question of whether or not a writing was part of the original apostolic message was the question of its orthodoxy. The central purpose in the fixing of the limits of scripture was to protect what was perceived as the orthodox Christian faith against heresy. It thus followed that any book that promoted Gnosticism, Marcionism or any other heretical doctrine could not be the work of an apostle: if it bore an apostle's name, it must be a forgery. Even the Gospel of John was suspect in some quarters up to the late second century because some of the things it said about Jesus and his mission seemed to have a Gnostic flavor. Also its references to the Holy Spirit leading the disciples into all truth (John 16:13) and the disciples being able to do greater things than Jesus (John 14:12) seemed to lend too much encouragement to the Montanists. On the other hand, a book like the Second Letter of Peter, which was almost certainly written long after Peter had died, was probably accepted because the Church at that time saw it as impeccably orthodox.

As late as the fourth century, the Letter to the Hebrews, which had been widely valued as scripture from early times, fell out of favor in the Western parts of the church. This was because of a problem being experienced in the Western churches at that particular time, the so-called "Donatist" controversy. In the severe persecution under the emperor Diocletian around 303 CE numerous Christians, including many clergy, had acceded to the demand to hand over their copies of the scriptures, and so effectively denied their faith. Later, when things became easier again, some people who came to be called the Donatists insisted that these people could not be recognized as priests. They refused to be in communion with churches that recognized them. The result of this was that they ended up not recognizing the majority of Christians, and they in turn were branded by the rest of the church as schismatic.

In this situation the mainstream church saw the letter to the Hebrews, with its statements about the impossibility of repentance after apostasy (Heb.2:2-3; 6:4-8; 10:26-31), as giving far too much ammunition to the Donatists, and so its orthodoxy became suspect. It is interesting that, more than a thousand years later, Luther was to have reservations about Hebrews because of these same passages: they seemed to take the ground away from the believer's assurance of being saved by grace without conditions.

The churches in the East, however, took a different view of it. The pressing problem for them was the prevalence of Arianism, a teaching that denied the divinity of Christ. In this context the letter to the Hebrews, with its clear statements about Jesus being the very image of God, different in kind from any angel, and at the same time completely human (Heb.1:2-4; 2:17-18 etc.), was much too valuable to neglect. Eventually the church in both the East and the West came to one mind about the letter to the Hebrews. With its strong theological content and the respect it had enjoyed from very early times, it was too good to lose. However, it was only accepted as part of scripture when some leading scholars (in the face of an almost complete lack of evidence!) asserted that it was written by Paul. To this day the fact that it comes at the end of Paul's letters, after the letters to

Timothy, Titus and Philemon, betrays that lingering doubt as to whether or not it was by Paul.

## The Books not Included

There is an enormous amount of literature from the early days of Christianity that never made it into the New Testament. In recent years there has been a lot of interest in "conspiracy" theories about how these writings were "suppressed" by the authorities of the Roman Catholic Church. These make a good story for those who love to read about conflict and corruption in high places (and few of us can resist that temptation!). However, the reality is more complex.

Certainly some writings were labeled as heretical and deliberately suppressed by the Church. However, we must remember that until the fourth century, when Christianity became an official religion under the patronage of the emperor Constantine, those who saw themselves as the guardians of orthodox Christianity were in no position to actually ban books and ensure that all copies were destroyed. By that time some had probably already disappeared because no one was interested in them any more. The canon of the New Testament, although it was not finalized until at least the end of the fourth century, had become roughly established by a wide consensus long before that. It was not as if until then large numbers of books were being popularly used as scripture, and then there was a major "cull". The mainstream church had long since come to the position of regarding certain books as scripture, and the list, though not yet exactly defined, was not much different from the New Testament as we now have it. Other books, some of which most Christians regarded as heretical, were being used in certain regions and churches: it was these that were largely condemned and destroyed once the Catholic Church had political power. Even then some of them survived, either because they were in the hands of sects that still flourished in spite of official disapproval, or because the Church authorities took some time to notice their heretical tendencies. The

Acts of John, for example, was much favored by the Manichees, a sect still quite active in the fifth century, and it was not finally condemned by the Catholic Church until the Second Council of Nicaea in 787. Even then it did not completely disappear: large parts of it have survived through excerpts found in other manuscripts.

The early Christian literature outside the New Testament may be divided into three categories. First, there are books of very early origin – contemporary with the New Testament books or slightly later – that were neither accepted into the New Testament nor rejected. They were widely read and valued with the approval of the Church authorities, but were never considered as scripture. Secondly, there are those at the other extreme, the books that were regarded as scripture by some people, but condemned by the mainstream church as heretical. Thirdly, there are those that are the most interesting from the point of view of the formation of the canon, the "borderline cases". These are books that were fairly widely recognized as scripture for a while, but when the Church began to define the canon of the New Testament more exactly, they were disputed and eventually excluded. They continued to be regarded as quite orthodox, but not as scripture.

In the first category were the letters of Ignatius. Ignatius was the third Bishop of Antioch, and he was taken under guard to Rome and died a martyr's death there in 107 CE. While on the way, he wrote seven letters, six of them to churches and one personal letter to Polycarp, the Bishop of Smyrna. In these letters he writes eloquently of the privilege of martyrdom, but at the same time he constantly emphasizes the need for Christians to submit completely to their bishops, elders and deacons. Part of the historical interest of these letters is the light they shed on the status of some of the New Testament writings at that time. Ignatius mentions one or two of the Gospels and some of the letters of Paul, but without any idea of their being holy scripture.

For him it is still the personal proclamation of the gospel that is central, and the authority to define true Christian belief is vested in the bishops as successors of the apostles. This set of letters was highly valued, but there was never any question of their being part of the New Testament.

There are other very early writings too – designed to present Christianity to interested outsiders, to refute heresy, or to edify and encourage Christians – that were valued and preserved. Some of them use material from the Gospels and other New Testament books, and what they add is simply embellishment or an imaginative setting for dialogue. One such is the anonymous Epistle to Diognetus, which is thought to date from the second or perhaps the third century. It is a strong apology for Christianity in opposition to paganism and Judaism. Another is the Epistula Apostolorum, a letter purporting to be from all twelve apostles, giving an account of a conversation between them and Jesus after his resurrection. It was meant as an exposition of orthodox doctrine against the second century Gnostics Simon and Cerinthus. It is evidently dependent on the New Testament Gospels, but with free adaptations and embellishments. The Acts of Pilate is an expanded story of the trial, crucifixion and resurrection of Jesus, and of a meeting of the Jewish council to inquire into the resurrection and ascension. It is possible, but not certain, that it was written as early as the mid second century.

Also in this category are some works of legend and fiction. Fiction based on the Bible has always been popular, and Church authorities have never tried to suppress it so long as it seemed harmless. In particular, Christians have always been fascinated by the birth and childhood of Jesus. Among the New Testament Gospels, only Matthew and Luke mention this part of the story, and even they tell us very little. However, there has been no shortage of imaginative writers willing to fill in the gaps. The most popular work of this type is the Protevangelium of James, written as early as the second century and claiming to be by

James, the brother of Jesus. It presumably survived because nothing in it was theologically controversial (at least until modern times, when the Immaculate Conception became an issue between Roman Catholics and Protestants). It harmonizes the nativity stories in Matthew and Luke, and adds many other embellishments which served to feed mediaeval piety and art. It is this book that tells us that Mary's parents were called Joachim and Anne, that she was immaculately conceived, that Joseph was an old man, that the people referred to as "brothers" of Jesus were Joseph's sons by a previous marriage, that Mary and Joseph rode to Bethlehem on a donkey, and that Jesus was born in a cave.

Another work in this vein is the Infancy Gospel of Thomas. This is a collection of stories about miracles performed by Jesus when he was a child. One of the best known is that he shaped birds out of clay and then made them come alive and fly. Other stories are nothing like as sweet at this: Jesus is seen as rather a naughty boy, playing some quite cruel tricks on people with his supernatural powers. This book, feeding as it did the popular desire for miracles and for aggressive "proof" of the superiority of Christ over rival faiths, was very popular in the Middle Ages. Its origin could be as early as the second century, though its attribution to Thomas is much later.

The only book in the New Testament that continues the story after the ministry of Jesus is the Acts of the Apostles. Here too there was a gap demanding to be filled. There are many books of "Acts" describing the exploits of the apostles, especially those hardly mentioned in the New Testament book, as they took the gospel to various remote parts of the world and performed spectacular miracles. Most of them were condemned as heretical, but one that was not condemned was the Acts of Paul and Thecla, a second-century account of journeys taken by Paul with a female companion who was converted at Iconium. One reason that this book was never rejected by the Church is probably that it portrays Thecla as a virgin, thus fitting in easily with the cult of asceticism and celibacy that caught on very early in Christian history. Some scholars think this book has a grain of historical truth in it, testifying to the importance of female missionaries in the early days, a theme that soon became suppressed with the development of the all-male hierarchy of the Church.

Imagination has also been brought to bear on gaps in the New Testament epistles. Some time in the second century there appeared the document later called 3 Corinthians, an imaginary letter from the church at Corinth to Paul, followed by Paul's reply. This was an attempt to fill in a gap implied by Paul's reference in 2 Corinthians to another letter (2 Cor.2:3-4). Similarly, Paul's letter to the Colossians mentions (4:16) a letter he wrote at the same time to Laodicea. Some time between the second and fourth centuries someone wrote "Paul's Letter to the Laodiceans", a work that remained popular for centuries. Neither of these works were condemned by the Church, because their theology was regarded as perfectly orthodox, and their attribution to Paul was always recognized as a pious fiction.

However, the great majority of early Christian gospels, "Acts" and epistles were rejected as scripture because they came from groups regarded as heretical. Sometimes this was not immediately recognized. The Gospel of Peter was probably written as early as the first century, and was in use in the churches of Syria about 200 CE. Serapion, the Bishop of Antioch, at first approved its use, but when he came to read it for himself he decided it was heretical and instructed his churches not to use it. This incident is interesting as evidence that even at that time the churches were not closed to the possibility of other gospels in addition to Matthew, Mark, Luke and John. Anything written by Peter was, in Serapion's mind, worthy to be read in churches as scripture. It was only when he had read it and found its content heretical that he concluded it must be a forgery. What this Gospel actually contained was completely unknown until the discovery of an eighth or ninth century manuscript at Akhmim, in Upper Egypt, in 1886/7, which appears to be that Gospel, though we cannot be certain. If it is, then we have evidence that it was still being copied six hundred years after Serapion banned its use in the churches of Syria. It seems to be confined largely to the death and resurrection of Jesus.

Probably the best known of all the gospels outside the New Testament is another late discovery, the Gospel of Thomas. Its existence was always known, but all we had of it was a few fragments of the Greek. However, a complete Coptic translation dating from the fourth century was discovered at Nag Hammadi, Egypt, in 1945. The gospel was probably written in the latter half of the first century. It could well have been one of the books banned by the Church authorities in the fourth century and deliberately buried so that it would not be found and burned. It was found together with other Gnostic writings, and it begins in typically Gnostic fashion: "These are the secret sayings which the living Jesus spoke and which Didymus Judas Thomas wrote down. And he said, 'Whoever finds the interpretation of these saying will not experience death'".

This introduction expresses a characteristic Gnostic view of Jesus as a teacher of secret wisdom, as opposed to the Church's view of him as primarily the Redeemer who died and rose again to save the world. The Gospel is purely a collection of sayings, with no narrative at all. Thomas was revered in Syria and sometimes thought to be the twin brother of Jesus (Thomas and Didymus are the Aramaic and Greek words for "twin"). This gospel shows every sign of being as close to the original history as any of the New Testament Gospels. Many of the sayings in it will be very familiar to anyone who knows the New Testament. Sometimes they are identical with those in the other Gospels, but at other times there is a clearly Gnostic slant in the way they are reported. In any case, any collection of sayings of Jesus without the story of his death and resurrection was suspect. Scholars have conjectured that a collection of sayings of Jesus (which they call

"Q") lies behind large parts of Matthew and Luke: if this existed, it could well have disappeared for that reason.

While Christianity was spreading widely in the Gentile world, there were still Jewish Christians who clung more closely to their traditions. We can see something of the conflict with them in the letters of Paul, where the "circumcision party" was often present in the churches. Eventually these people seem to have divided from the others and become labeled Ebionites. They took part in most of the Jewish rituals, attending the Temple while it still stood, but they did not participate in animal sacrifices because they believed the death of Jesus had fulfilled their purpose and rendered them redundant. Since meat at that time was almost universally associated with sacrifice, this meant that they did not eat meat. There was a Gospel of the Ebionites, which was apparently an adaptation of material from Mark, Matthew and Luke, but omitting all references to Jesus eating meat or fish, because they believed he too was vegetarian.

These are only a few of the numerous writings that came to be rejected as heretical. Apart from the temporary acceptance of the Gospel of Peter in Syria, there is no evidence that there was any chance of any of them becoming part of the New Testament. We must remember, however, that to the communities who produced and used them, sometimes for a very long time, they were holy scripture.

We now come to the third category, the books that functioned as scripture for a time but were eventually excluded. One such work is the Epistle of Barnabas, a letter from the time of the Emperor Hadrian (117-138 CE), attributed to Barnabas because of its encouraging tone (see Acts 4:36). It is very reminiscent of the Epistle to the Hebrews, but much more extreme in its allegorical interpretation of all the Old Testament laws as referring directly to Christ. It remained popular for centuries, and was often bound up with New Testament manuscripts.

Another was the First Epistle of Clement to the Corinthians

(known as 1 Clement). It is a letter from the church in Rome to the church in Corinth. Its author is not named, but was always assumed to be Clement, the second or third Bishop of Rome. It was written about 96 CE, in response to a situation of conflict and rebellion in Corinth, and is a plea for Christian love and humility. Its tone indicates that by this time the Church at Rome was already beginning to see itself in a position of leadership in relation to other churches.

The Shepherd, by Hermas, was written in the early second century, reputedly by the brother of Pius, Bishop of Rome. It is the longest of all the early Christian writings, and recounts visions and messages given to Hermas by angels, one of whom appears in the form of a shepherd. It was valued very largely for its strong ethical content, and as late as the fourth century the question of its scriptural status was still being discussed. It was eventually excluded because it was not the work of an apostle. Another book of visions was the Apocalypse of Peter, written in the early second century. This tells how the disciples meet the risen Jesus on the Mount of Olives and ask him for further explanation about the world to come. They are then taken on a tour of heaven and hell. This story inspired many others in later times, notably Dante's *Divine Comedy*. However, although its scriptural status was apparently still being discussed in the fourth century, and it was being read in Syria in the fifth century, it eventually disappeared. It is now known only by some fragments discovered in 1886/7.

Another strong candidate for the New Testament that disappeared was the Didache, or Teaching of the Twelve Apostles. This was probably written before 100 CE and was quoted in the Epistle of Barnabas and other early writings. It is an outline of Christian morality, followed by instructions about baptism and Eucharist. For a long time it was known only through fragments, but a complete manuscript of the original was discovered in Istanbul in 1873. This manuscript is dated 1056, which means that it was only

since that date at the earliest that the work had fallen out of use
and ceased to be copied. Why this happened is not known, but it
could be that by that time the Catholic Church had so developed
its own rules and rituals around the sacraments that the Didache
was no longer wanted: where it agreed with current practice, it
was superfluous, and where it differed it was something of an
embarrassment.

The whole story of the selecting of the books of the New
Testament is clouded in uncertainty. It seems that the question as
such was not discussed until the fourth century. A kind of sifting
out was taking place, and most of the books were becoming
universally accepted while others were valued by certain parts of
the Church. Others, again, were being either condemned or just
quietly dropped by consensus. It is not until the fourth century
that we find people such as Eusebius and Athanasius specifically
discussing which books are acceptable as scripture.

It is also difficult to see just how firmly the decision (if we can
call it that) was made even at the end of the fourth century. In the
tenth century there were still at least six different New Testament
lists circulating in the Eastern churches. The evidence of ancient
copies of the Bible is also very confusing, For instance, the Codex
Claromontanus, a sixth-century manuscript discovered at
Clermont, France, omits Philippians, 1 and 2 Thessalonians and
Hebrews, but includes Hermas, the Acts of Paul and the
Apocalypse of Peter. This could imply a different version of the
canon. On the other hand it could be a matter of accidental
omission, since the status of Philippians and 1 Thessalonians had
never been in question. It could also be that the producers of
manuscript Bibles were not making a declaration as to which
books were in the Bible, but simply including books they thought
were wanted at that time. Paul's Letter to the Laodiceans, for
example, was included in a number of manuscript Bibles
throughout the Middle Ages. It may be that in an age when the
only people who could read the Bible were the educated clergy,

there was no need to show clearly which books were canonical and which were not, because the readers already knew. It was only when the Bible started being read by lay people that it became important to be clear about which books were in it.

## Have we the Right Selection?

The historical circumstances of the shaping of the New Testament have left us with an untidy mixture. This was inevitable. The four Gospels had to be kept as they were, complete with inconsistencies and contradictions, because their authenticity – their apostolic origin – was generally agreed. To choose one as the standard and reject the other three was not an option, because all four were respected and used in many parts of the Church. To tinker with them in order to iron out inconsistencies would be an admission that the Church did not fully accept the witness of the apostles. Tatian's Diatessaron, though it was popular for several centuries, never gained complete acceptance as scripture for this reason. The whole point the orthodox leaders were making was that they had kept the *original* teaching intact.

The situation was the same with the other writings. Certain letters were generally agreed to have been written by Paul, the specially ordained apostle to the Gentiles. At the same time, there were other letters that bore the names of some of the Twelve – James, Peter, John and Jude. Modern scholarship doubts the authenticity of any of these, but in the period when these controversies were taking place they were generally agreed to be genuine, and the Church could not let go of any document that was believed to be the work of an apostle. We today may think it would have been more convenient if the New Testament consisted of a plain, systematic summary of the Christian faith sanctioned by the authority of the Church. At that time, however, such a document would have had no authority. The only way the Church could assert its authenticity was by holding on to whatever documents *happened to exist* that could be claimed as "apostolic", even if some of them had very little to contribute to Christian understanding.

And so the New Testament that was fixed between the second and fourth centuries of the Christian era was not an ideal theological construction. It was a response to the pressures of the time, and was the only selection possible in the circumstances. The Bible itself is, like many of its parts, an entity that was never planned and designed as a whole but grew by the accumulation of a number of *ad hoc* creations. This fact was, in a sense, acknowledged as early as the writings of Papias around 100 CE. Talking of Mark's Gospel being based on the memoirs of Peter, he says: "Peter did not intend to give a complete exposition of the Lord's ministry, but delivered his instructions to meet the needs of the moment. It follows, then, that Mark was guilty of no blunder if he wrote, simply to the best of his recollections, an incomplete account."

This principle could well be applied to most of the Bible. Its writings were for "the needs of the moment", and so was the final selection of its contents. In view of the way it evolved and the purpose it was meant to serve, we cannot expect it to be a complete and balanced account of Christian history or doctrine. At the same time we may ask: is this selection of writings, worked out by the Church in a very different age from ours, in the midst of controversies that are no longer our concern, the right one to be scripture for us today? Are all the books that seemed essential to Christians in those early days really essential for us? Are there books they rejected that we could find really useful?

When we look at the criteria by which books were selected or de-selected for the New Testament, we have to say that, strictly speaking, and *on the basis of its own criteria*, the Church did not get it right. The claims to *apostolic authorship*, for instance, are hardly tenable today for many of the New Testament writings. Most scholars agree that some of the letters attributed to Paul were more probably written after Paul's death by people who followed his general teaching and wanted to claim Paul's authority for what they taught. The Letters to Timothy and Titus, and the Letter to the Ephesians, are most probably in this category. Many scholars also include in it the Letter to the Colossians and the second Letter to the Thessalonians. As far as the other New Testament letters are concerned, 1 Peter is not generally thought to have been written by the apostle, and on 2 Peter scholarly opinion is virtually unanimous that it was written some time in the second century, long after the death of all the apostles. There is doubt too about all the others.

As far as the Gospels are concerned, it is now generally agreed that they are the product of a generation or two of handed-down and adapted traditions. It is highly unlikely that Matthew and John could be the work of the men of those names listed among the twelve. It is much more likely that, in the form in which we have them, they are the end result of traditions that developed within churches that looked back to those apostles as their founders or chief sources of authority. All this means that the New Testament as modern scholars view it is nowhere near as "apostolic" as we used to think. If today we applied a strict criterion of apostolic authorship, we would have even less of a New Testament than that proposed by Marcion!

The criterion of orthodoxy can also be questioned today. We have already seen that many parts of the Bible – mainly in the Old Testament, but some in the New Testament too – are problematic and hardly consistent with what many Christians today believe. The early centuries of Christian history were a very different age from ours. Ways of life and perceptions of the world have radically changed since then. How can we say that the canon of scripture formed then can express our understanding of essential Christianity today?

Questions like these have prompted some people to ask whether the canon of scripture should be revised. It was, after all, the Church that defined it, so is it not within the power of the Church to change it? This seems a logical question, but when we look at it more closely we can see that in fact it is largely an academic question.

People have sometimes talked of a "canon within the canon". That is, they have suggested that the canon of scripture should somehow be pruned of all its "non-genuine", "inauthentic" or "sub-Christian" accretions until only the "genuine" or "authentic" core remains. Apart from the impossibility of getting even two people to agree as to what this authentic core consists of, there is behind this idea the assumption that somewhere within this mixed-up conglomeration of writings there is a core that is perfect and infallible. This of course is basically a fundamentalist idea disguised in the clothes of biblical criticism. The point of rejecting the fundamentalism that makes the Bible infallible is that the *whole* of it is a human book about God. Every bit of the Bible is imperfect because it is the product of human minds. At the same time, this does not prevent us believing that it is inspired in so far as it is the product of the Holy Spirit. If we believe that God chooses to work along with imperfect human beings, then we can surely believe that God can speak through the Bible with all its imperfections, and not just through some small part of it that is perfect.

Turning our backs on fundamentalism releases us from the obligation to believe everything we read in the Bible just because it is in the Bible. It thus ceases to be a matter of supreme importance whether a certain passage is "genuine" scripture or not. We would be unlikely to stop believing something because it had been decided that the book in which we found it was not supposed to be in the Bible after all, and we would be just as unlikely to start believing some new doctrine because of a book being added to the Bible.

It would in any case be impossible in practice for the canon of scripture to be changed. Who would do it? If the Pope declared a revised canon, this would not be recognized by Protestants or the Eastern Orthodox. If the World Council of Churches did it, there are plenty of Christians who do not recognize the authority of that body, especially on issues concerning scripture. Just as, strictly speaking, the canon of scripture was never fixed by the Christian Church acting as a whole, so it would be impossible today for the Christian Church to act as a whole in changing it.

Not only would it be impossible, it would be inappropriate too. Whatever the ups and downs of the story of the formation of the canon of scripture, whatever the doubts expressed about certain books, however long the process took, the Bible is now a fact of history. The work of all the great Christian theologians, the liturgy of all the churches and the devotions of countless Christians have been based on the assumption that these books were holy scripture. All this cannot now be taken away. We may criticize the Bible on historical grounds, question its relevance for our age, or disagree with many of its ethical and theological assumptions, but we cannot undo the historical fact that it is the Christian Bible.

What we can and must do is ask questions about the Bible's real relationship to Christian faith. As we have seen, the Bible was never designed to be a concise, systematic statement of Christian doctrine or ethics. Down through the ages it has nourished the Christian faith and the devotional life of believers. It has been material for the preaching of the faith. It has inspired Christians to hold on to their faith, or challenged them to think afresh about it. It has often been regarded as an authority for the defining of the faith, though usually in a negative sense, defining what Christians should *not* believe or should *not* do. However, the Bible is not Christianity. It is not identical with the Christian faith, nor is it the source of faith. It is a phenomenon that has existed throughout Christian history alongside and in close relation to the Christian faith itself.

## Historical Accident?

From one point of view we can of course see the whole process of selection as a chain of historical accidents. Chance always plays a role. Chance played a role in what things were written. As we have already seen, some of the letters Paul wrote included things that he would not have written if he had been able to visit a particular church at that time and say those things to the people face to face. Similarly, chance inevitably played a role in the decisions that shaped the canon.

Not only was it a matter of chance, it was also sometimes a matter of human faults and weaknesses. The champions of what became the "orthodox" Christian faith were not entirely pure in their motives. They were probably less intelligent and creative than some of the "heretics". Like most church leaders throughout history, their main concern was shepherding the flock, trying to keep things in order, and silencing anyone who threatened to rock the boat. As the Church became more powerful and prosperous, motives of downright greed and ambition often influenced the theological controversies. It could cynically be said that what we see today as orthodox Christian faith is only the views of those who were lucky enough to be on the winning side. It may be that, but for some accidents of history, we might all have been Marcionites, Gnostics or Arians today.

However, the emergence of orthodox Christianity as it has been known throughout Christian history is more than just an accident. There was a kind of inevitability about it. We could say that it is largely the result of the evolutionary principle of "the survival of the fittest". Christianity as a strong institution embracing so many classes and cultures, and surviving so many deep changes in the course of world history, in some ways had to be as it is. For the most part, the "heresies" died because they did not have the power to last, and the beliefs that survived as "orthodoxy" did so because they were the kind of beliefs that made possible a structured church with the adaptability and stamina to survive.

If, for instance, the absolute uniqueness and centrality of Jesus had been set aside, the memory of him and his teaching might have survived as part of the general wisdom of humanity, but there would not have been a Christian Church as such. If the principle of universality had been lost – if the Church had remained strictly Jewish, or if it had followed the Gnostic idea of a spiritual elite – there could never have been a Church embracing and shaping the various nations of Europe and then spreading out to the whole world. On the other hand, while refusing to remain within Judaism, the mainstream church insisted on retaining its roots in the Jewish tradition and recognizing the Jewish scriptures. This gave Christianity a solid historical base. We could also say that the inevitable tension in the relationship between the Testaments has probably given Christianity a challenge that has kept it fresh and constantly renewable. Moreover, the retention of the Jewish scriptures helped Christianity maintain the fundamentally ethical nature of religion. Even though Christians believe that Jesus is "the end of the Law", the Law is still there, somehow holding us back from that misunderstanding of grace that worried the writer of the Epistle of James and tended to appear from time to time in Gnostic teaching – the idea that if you are "spiritual" it doesn't matter how you behave.

The insistence on the reality of the Incarnation – that Jesus was a real human being – probably owed much of its importance in the early days to the martyrs who lost their lives in the various times of persecution. When believers were constantly in danger of a death that was all too real, there was enormous strength and inspiration to be drawn from the example of Jesus himself. There quickly developed a theology of martyrdom centered on the cross. Any threat to the reality of the death of Jesus was a threat to that theology. It was also true that the blood of the martyrs was the seed of the church: it was the church of the martyrs that survived and grew. It is perhaps significant that when the Church becomes accepted as part of the establishment, the idea of the fleshly reality of Jesus tends to be played down. Many people in Christendom have tended to regard Jesus as a god rather than a man – to imagine him as always being spotlessly clean and floating a little way off the ground with a visible halo over his head. A church that has to cope with the harsh realities of human life soon finds that only a real human, flesh and blood Jesus can be good news.

And so it could be said that there was something inevitable about certain kinds of belief becoming central while others died out or were banished to the fringes. The principles that survived were in fact the only ones by which Christianity could have survived and become a great world religion. They are also principles that are still central to the faith of most Christians today, though they may express them in a very different way.

There are some principles of traditional orthodox Christianity that are questioned by many people today: for example, the hierarchical structure of the Church, the acceptance of class divisions in society, and the predominant role of men in leadership. Some of the "heresies" of the early days included alternative thinking on some of these issues, and we could say it is regrettable that they were suppressed or failed to survive. On the other hand, from what we know of the books that were rejected as heretical, they would not have been an unmixed blessing to us today if they had become part of scripture. For example, those writings that stressed the importance and independent activity of women also tended to set up virginity and extreme asceticism as an ideal and show an exaggerated contempt for the flesh. Similarly, documents like the Gospel of Thomas perhaps convey more of the provocative, paradoxical, "teasing" character of the teaching of Jesus than has been preserved in the mainstream tradition, but at the same time they seem to present an elitist spirituality that excludes the great majority of ordinary people from full access to salvation.

Some of these minority types of Christianity have turned out to be quite resilient, appearing at various times in history in different forms – social radicalism, celibate communities, non-hierarchical churches, mystical and non-dogmatic spirituality, and so on. Some of them have been part of the variety displayed within the established churches (for example, monasticism), others have broken away from the mainstream church or been excluded from it. Minority views that have a strong appeal, whether good or bad, have a tendency to keep reappearing, and the suppression or acceptance of some of their scriptures in the past makes little actual difference in the present..

Ironically, in fixing this particular selection of books and vesting authority in it, the Church has kept things like the preaching of the Hebrew prophets and the teachings of Jesus, which include radical challenges to society and to the Church itself. This means that conventional orthodoxy can always be challenged on the authority of that very Bible the orthodox Church authorities have sanctioned. This has been done by St. Francis of Assisi, John Wyclif, the Levelers, the Quakers, modern liberation theologians and numerous others in the course of history. Perhaps the most ironic example of this comes out of the history of the transatlantic slave trade. The slave masters taught their slaves to read the Bible because they thought it would make them behave better, but when they read the Bible they found in it the story of God setting the Hebrew slaves free and leading them to the promised land, and they developed a spirituality of their own based on that story.

However, some of these alternative forms of Christianity face the same problem as the early "heresies": an inability to survive for long in the realities of the world. This does not of course make them wrong. One could equally say that orthodox, conventional Christianity has deserted its roots and made itself too comfortable in the world.

The traditional orthodox Christianity we have inherited, with its fixed canon of scripture, is not perfect, but at the same time we can recognize that there was something inevitable about it, and it is not merely an accident of history.

# 5. WHERE IS THE REAL AUTHORITY?

Anyone whose life is lived in the public eye, whether a member of the royal family, a television personality, or just someone who has a prominent position in the local community, is well aware of the vulnerability of his or her situation. A pedestal can be a prison. The public who put you on it are determined to keep you on it – unless you disappoint them, in which case they will take great pleasure in pulling you down from it. You are either all good or all bad. Your life is public property, and you are never allowed really to be yourself. The same thing happens when writings become "holy scripture". Subtle changes take place in the way they are read. They lose something of their original meaning and acquire a new meaning. Though revered as an authority, they are no longer truly themselves but someone else's property.

## Authority means Distortion
One of the first things that happens is that the history behind the writings, and their original function in their setting, tends to be forgotten. If the writings are understood as God's direct word to the whole of humanity, the particularity of their history becomes unimportant. The drama of history is flattened out, and they become the timeless "oracles of God".

When we, with our modern mentality, study an ancient text we try to find out first what the original writer meant to say. We use whatever we know of the historical and cultural background to find out what the words meant at the time, who the writer was addressing, what were the issues at stake, and what was the purpose of saying those things at that particular time. Once we have built up a picture of what the original writer really meant, we then go on to ask the separate question of what relevance this might have for us today. For Jews and Christians in pre-modern times, and indeed for many devout Bible readers today, the difference between these two questions hardly arises. If it is God who speaks through the scriptures, their message is for the present reader. There is therefore no hesitation in violating what historians would see as the original meaning and assuming that it refers directly to one's own situation.

In the same way, because the text is read as divine revelation rather than literature, differences of style are not noticed. This is why it was possible for many generations of believers to accept without question that Solomon wrote the book of Ecclesiastes. To us, with our modern sense of historical perspective and practice of literary criticism, it seems highly unlikely that an Israelite king in the tenth century BCE could have said those things in that kind of way. The ideas, and the style in which they are expressed, obviously belong centuries later, in the skeptical, philosophical culture of the Greek-speaking world after the conquests of Alexander. But the devout believer, to whom every word of it is holy scripture, is not looking at style.

"Holy scripture" is assumed to be completely true and consistent with itself. If some historical statements within it contradict others, this is often hardly noticed, because people are not reading the scripture with that kind of question in mind. If the discrepancy does come to their attention, the devout reader puts it down to the inability of human minds to grasp divine mysteries. When different theological or moral ideas are expressed in the different parts of scripture, it is assumed that they are simply different facets of the truth. The reader does not accept the possibility that the different authors might have actually disagreed with one another. Again, the history – the living process of argument and conflict that lies behind the writings – fades into the background.

Seeing a set of writings as holy scripture also has a distorting effect on the relative importance of passages. If it is all "holy scripture", then every sentence within it is felt to have equal value. A single sentence from anywhere in it can be quoted as an authoritative divine oracle. Devout believers often only experience their scripture one "text" at a time. They are hardly aware of the flow of a whole book or even a whole chapter. Paradoxically, though fundamentalists are often upset by the way modern scholars break up a book (like Isaiah for instance) into separate parts, they themselves often break up every book in the Bible even more, because they read it as a collection of individual "texts", each one a separate divine oracle. The most trivial sentence, a writer's off-the-cuff remark, becomes a "verse", which in itself is a precious unit of divine truth. Sermons have no doubt been preached on Paul leaving his cloak behind in Troas (2 Tim.4:13).

At the same time, once the infallibility of scripture becomes a controversial issue, as it is today, some quite unimportant passages attract far more attention than they deserve. For example, when Jesus is talking about how David went into the temple with his men and ate the sacred bread, the words are added: "when Abiathar was high priest" (Mark 2:26). This is a simple historical mistake. The priest concerned in the incident was Ahimelech, Abiathar's father. Abiathar became a companion of David and his band of outlaws a little later. Later still, when David had established himself as king in Jerusalem, Abiathar and Zadok jointly were the leading priests, but even then the expression "high priest" is not used (see 1 Sam.21:1; 22:20; 2 Sam.15:24 etc.). There was obviously a natural human slip of memory, either by Jesus as he said the words, or by the person who wrote them down. Considering that the scriptures at that time were available only in manuscript scrolls, with no chapter and verse divisions, and no such thing as a concordance, it is hardly surprising that little slips like this would happen.

Matthew and Luke obviously spotted the mistake in Mark: in their versions the words are omitted (Matt.12:4; Luke 6:4). The whole question is quite trivial, and does not affect the point that Jesus was making in the slightest. However, for those who claim that the Bible – every word of it – is infallibly true, these few words are a difficulty that has to be explained. And so reams of paper have been expended on discussing a phrase that really has no bearing on the message of Jesus at all!

Perhaps the most glaring example of this distortion in relative importance is the little book of Jonah. It is a book everyone has heard of for the wrong reason. Virtually every believing Jew or Christian has at some time been drawn into an argument about whether Jonah really was swallowed and regurgitated by a great fish. The real treasures of the book – the important questions it raises about judgment and mercy, the profundity of its message about God's love for all living things, even its delightful touches of humor – are ignored and unappreciated while people argue about the fish. We could say that, whether that fish existed or not, it was definitely a red herring!

## Which Guiding Principle?

Another thing that happens when a set of writings becomes holy scripture is that it is assumed to have a single purpose, and every-thing in it is interpreted in line with that purpose. There is a particular "slant" put upon its interpretation by the community whose scripture it is.

For the orthodox Jew, the heart of scripture is the first five books, "the Law". Everything in those books, whether it looks like a law or not, tends to be interpreted as law. The prophets and the other writings are meant to comment on the Law, illustrate it, and exhort us to obey it. This perception of scripture led on into the rabbinical tradition that is familiar to us from the Gospels, and which predominated in Judaism especially after the fall of Jerusalem. The rabbis pored over the sacred writings, trying to achieve consistency where it seemed to be lacking, and constantly arguing about their meaning. Questions were asked about the nature and ways of God and the practical application of the commandments, and answers were found somewhere in the sacred writings. There was a great accumulation of interpretations and rulings by renowned scholars – a kind of "case law". The scriptures were assumed to be primarily about *how God's people should behave.*

The early Christians drew on a different tradition of interpretation that had developed in some Jewish sects of the time, notably those associated with the Dead Sea Scrolls. While the rabbis saw the scripture as *law*, the Christians saw it as *prophecy.* Traditional Jewish belief had certainly seen the scriptures as containing predictions, but what was new was the idea that the *whole* of scripture was fundamentally a prediction of one particular set of events. For the Dead Sea Scrolls people, this was the life and situation of their community. For Christians it was the life, death and resurrection of Jesus. Scripture, in the mind of Christians, was *the revelation given by God to prepare the way for Christ.*

There is thus a difference in the meaning of the word "prophet" between Judaism and Christianity. For the Jews at the time of Jesus, a prophet was primarily an expounder of the divine Law, while for the Christians a prophet was a foreteller of the future. These two different perceptions of the role of a prophet, as we have seen, lie behind the different order of the Jewish scriptures and the Christian Old Testament. In the Jewish Bible the prophets, being the interpreters of the Torah, follow the Torah itself, and the other writings (Psalms, Proverbs etc.) come as a further interpretation of the Law. In the Christian Old Testament the prophets, being the predictors, come as a kind of climax at the end.

A little later Christians began to look at their own writings in a way that was already being used by some people in interpreting the Jewish scriptures: scripture was seen as *divine wisdom*. For Jews and for Christians in the Hellenistic world, there was a need to show that the faith they held was not some eccentric backwoods idea that sophisticated Greeks could afford to laugh at. It was just as intellectually respectable, just as ancient (an important consideration in that culture) and just as spiritually refined as anything the Greek philosophers had produced. The scriptures were a rich repository of spiritual wisdom. However, there was the problem of all those parts of scripture that did not easily lend themselves to such a reading – ordinary stories of ordinary people, detailed descriptions of ritual, even earthy and doubtfully ethical passages. It seemed that the only way through this problem was to read the scriptures allegorically, seeing through the earthly exterior to the heavenly message encoded in them.

The Greeks themselves had actually begun this process. Philosophers were exploring the fundamental nature of the universe with the new-found tools of logical thought, but at the same time Greek culture had not let go of the gods and all the myths and legends about them. The answer was to read these stories as symbolic representations of philosophical truth. The Jewish writer Philo of Alexandria, around the time of Christ, had begun to do this with the Hebrew scriptures. Christian apologists followed this example, and eventually the Christian writings that were also coming to be regarded as holy scripture began to be treated in the same way.

The leading light in this process was Origen (c. 195-254 CE). His principle was that literal interpretation should be avoided, not so much because of the historical problems and contradictions (though Origen was aware of these) but mainly because the literal meaning of a text could be spiritually unhelpful, coarse or even morally objectionable. Interestingly, Origen and his contemporaries saw the same problems that we today see in the Bible, but dealt with them in quite a different way. From their point of view, every word of the Bible was divinely inspired, and if the literal meaning was not satisfactory, then it must have been inspired with a different purpose – a higher spiritual meaning that must be sought out by the spiritually discerning reader.

Origen and others often found a number of different levels of meaning in a text. These were generally resolved into four. First there was the *literal* meaning, which might or might not be helpful. Then there was the *spiritual* (or allegorical) meaning, seeing in the text a symbolic representation of some article of belief or theological principle. Thirdly, there was the *moral* meaning, pointing the reader to general principles about living the virtuous life. Finally there was the *anagogical* meaning. This word comes from a Greek word which means "leading up": this meaning of the text would lead the reader up into heavenly realms and eternal mysteries. It could also be called *eschatological*, pointing to the ultimate things and to life beyond death.

This kind of interpretation often led to texts being forced to mean something quite unrelated to what they had originally meant. A well known example of this is Origen's interpretation of the parable of the Good Samaritan (Luke 10:29-37). He sees the man traveling down the road from Jerusalem to Jericho as Adam, the representative of all human beings, descending from the Celestial City to the sinful world. The robbers are the demons and the false doctrines that came before Christ. The wounds are disobedience and sin. The theft of the man's clothing represents his being robbed of the garment of immortality and all the virtues, and his being left "half dead" is an exact picture of humanity: the soul is immortal but the body is mortal. The priest is the Law and the Levite is the prophets, both unable to help him. The Samaritan is Christ, and the beast of burden is the body of Christ that bears our sins. The wine is the word of his teaching, and the oil his compassion. The inn is the Church, and the innkeeper represents the apostles and the bishops. The Samaritan's promise to return is the promise of the return of

Christ.

This is often quoted today as an example of how *not* to handle the Bible, but, incredibly, there are still preachers who seriously use it. No doubt many devout Christians down through the ages have drawn inspiration from this understanding of the story. However, when we read the parable within its context it seems fairly obvious that it was meant as a simple story to get the teacher of the law who was interrogating Jesus to face an uncomfortable answer to his own question, *"who is my neighbor?"* Interpreting it as a complicated allegory of sin and salvation is not only silly, but can actually be a harmful diversion, because it blunts the sharp moral challenge of the story.

The other problem with allegorical interpretation is that it makes it virtually impossible to fix the "real" meaning. If a text never means just what it seems to mean, who is to say what it does mean? Allegory can make anything mean anything. To the postmodern thinking of today, this hardly matters. Any text is open to a wide range of interpretations: it means what the reader sees in it. This may be a valid understanding when the text in question is an ordinary piece of literature, but when it is seen as an "authority", an infallible set of directions for correct doctrine and behavior, it becomes a problem. How can a text have authority over us when it can mean whatever we want it to mean?

In practice, Origen's principle was to say that scripture, being God's word, must always be consistent with itself and with the Christian faith. But this brings us up against the really big question: what is the Christian faith, and who says so? Some of the ways in which Origen and others interpreted the Bible are quite alien to what Christians of today think. What they saw as basic Christian belief was often only a reflection of their own culture. Origen's belief, for instance, was heavily influenced by the Platonic philosophy that was virtually an unquestioned assumption in the culture of his time. To people of that culture, it was an undisputed fact that there are two worlds, the material and the spiritual, that the spiritual is superior, and that everything we see in the material world is a mere shadow of the real thing that exists in the spiritual world. It was equally unquestioned – plain "fact" – that man represents the rational spirit and woman represents the flesh. It is assumptions like this that make Origen's interpretation of scripture alien and sometimes offensive to us, but to him they were part of the "common sense" package of Christianity that guided Christians into a sound interpretation of the Bible. He had no more reason to doubt them than the Victorian missionaries had to doubt their assumption that Christian morality was identical with bourgeois European manners.

As time went on the answer to the question "who is to say what scripture really means?" was inevitably given in terms of ecclesiastical authority. Starting with the simple common sense principle that, since the Bible is Christian scripture, Christians are the ones who best understand what it means, the Church soon developed a more formal and rigid principle: the Bible is the Church's book, therefore the only correct interpretation of it is that given by the Church. The next logical step was to identify the Church with those who were in charge in the Church, and then with the one person ultimately in charge, the Pope. In mediaeval Roman Catholicism there was no distinction in practice between the authority of the Bible and the tradition of the Church. The Church was Christ's body on earth, therefore what the Church believed and taught was true. Anyone who questioned the Church on the basis of what the Bible said was simply a heretic. How could the Bible possibly be understood to say something in opposition to the teaching of the Church? They were both part of the same absolute authority, and there could be no inconsistency between them. This led to the ironic situation that scripture now had virtually no authority: the authority was the Church.

There were some people in mediaeval Christendom who saw a difference between the teaching and practice of the Church in their time and the gospel of Christ as it was in the beginning. St. Francis of Assisi embarked on a radically different way of life as he drew his inspiration directly from the teachings of Jesus, but he did this with no thought of questioning the authority of the Church. Others, however, like John Wycliffe in England and Jan Hus in Bohemia, began to view some aspects of the contemporary church as alien to the New Testament. Eventually the movement known as the Reformation that started with Martin Luther in the sixteenth century decisively rejected the notion that only the Church has the authority to define the meaning of scripture. By that time many people saw a glaring inconsistency between true Christianity and the things done by the Church in the name of Christ. It was clear to them that Church tradition and scripture were not necessarily in agreement. And so was born one of the emotive slogans of the Reformation: "scripture alone". The Bible, they claimed, was the authority to which the Church must bow and by which it must be judged.

In making this assertion, the Reformers rejected allegorical interpretation. There had already been reservations about this within traditional Catholicism. The great theologian Thomas Aquinas in the thirteenth century had asserted that whatever allegorical meanings could be found in the Bible it was only the literal meaning that could be used as authority for settling doctrinal issues. The Reformers stressed this even more. They argued that if God gave us the Bible so that we would know what is necessary to salvation, then all we need to know must be there before us in its plain meaning. It should not need clever theologians or other-worldly mystics to draw out the "true" meaning. As Tyndale put it, the boy plowing the field, if he can read the Bible in his own language, will know the way of salvation.

## The Church's Book, or Anybody's?

We sometimes forget that this principle, that anyone could read the Bible and interpret it for themselves, was dependent on a technological development: the invention of the printing press which, as far as Europe was concerned, came about in the mid fifteenth century. We take so many things for granted about the Bible today. We can buy one in the local book shop. We can keep one by our bedside for daily reading. We can organize a study group and ask people to bring their own Bibles. All these things were unknown concepts before the invention of printing. Printing changed the physical nature of the Bible. Until its invention, all Bibles were handwritten, and therefore very heavy and very expensive. They were also, in Western Europe at least, all in Latin, and only a select few could read anyway. This meant that in those days the great majority of Christian believers never actually *read* the Bible at all. The priests in their sermons told them what was in it, they learned catechisms and songs, they saw the pictures and statues in the churches, and they watched passion plays, but they never actually *read* the Bible.

The advent of printing led to the spread of literacy and the production of books in the language of ordinary people rather than in Latin. This meant that the Bible was no longer the property of the clergy. Ordinary people could buy a Bible, read it and understand it for themselves, and Protestantism positively encouraged them to do so. This, however, led to a development that most of the Reformers would not have welcomed: an explosion of different interpretations that eventually became a kind of "free for all". Lutherans, Presbyterians, Independents, Baptists, Quakers and Unitarians all claimed to base their beliefs and practices on scripture, and the number of different sects continued to increase, and is still increasing today. It has been said that today there are as many "denominations" as there are verses in the Bible! "Plain meaning" or not, the Bible could be read in as many different ways as there were people to read it.

This had two other profound effects. The first was a growth in the idea of the Bible as a source of guidance and inspiration for the *individual*. In the age of print, reading is a solitary activity.

Whether we are literally alone or not, reading is essentially a meeting between two: myself and the book in my hand. This individual relationship with the Bible is quite different from the relationship people had with it before the invention of printing. If we look back to the very origins of the Bible, we find that most of it was meant for community use. The laws and stories in the Hebrew scriptures were read in public or repeated in the liturgy. The Psalms were meant to be sung by the congregation. The Gospel stories were told and re-told in the Christian communities when they met for worship. Paul's letters to the churches were delivered through messengers and read to the congregation. Down through Christian history most people's experience of the Bible was one of having it read to them when they congregated for worship.

Once the invention of printing and the spread of literacy had made Bible reading a personal thing, this in turn encouraged the idea of religion itself as a personal thing. Talk of accepting Jesus as one's own "personal" Lord and Savior became part of evangelical tradition. In wider circles too it came to be taken for granted that a person's religion is a private matter between them and God. This would seem very strange to the devotees of most religions throughout history, for whom religion has been essentially a community activity.

The other effect was the separation of the Bible from the ministry and preaching of the Church. Before the invention of printing, the Bible and the Church were inseparable, not just in theology but in everyday experience. The only Bibles that existed were in churches and monasteries. Scholars read the Bible in the libraries of universities, but the universities themselves were dominated by the Church. The only access people had to the Bible was through the Church. However, once people were able to handle and read their own copy of the Bible their perception of it changed. It became a free standing entity, cut off from its roots in the Church.

This was not necessarily the intention of the first Reformers: they seem to have been mainly concerned that people should read the Bible so as to have immediate access to what it said and not be tied to what the clergy told them. It was assumed that this reading took place within the life of the Church, and that the Bible was interpreted within the framework of generally accepted Christian belief and practice. However, once the process began there was no stopping it. Even very ancient, universal practices and beliefs came to be questioned on the basis of the Bible. The Anabaptists opposed the baptism of new-born infants that had been virtually universal practice for at least a thousand years. They also questioned the assumption that had existed since Constantine that religion must be regulated by the state. The Unitarians went further, and asserted that the Trinity was not a biblical doctrine. The Quakers challenged the whole concept of church buildings, sacraments, creeds and ordained ministry. There arose the concept of "universal apostasy" – the idea that the Church throughout its entire history has been off course, and that "we are" – or even in some cases "I am"! – the first to see what the Bible really teaches. One effect of this is that generations of Protestants have been brought up with a close familiarity with the Bible, but virtually no knowledge of Church history between the end of Acts and the founding of their own denomination.

In Protestant piety the Bible increasingly came to be seen as the source and content of faith, the thing that Christians above all believe in. Some people started calling themselves "Bible Christians", feeling this to be a more appropriate badge of true Christianity than anything that suggested church or sacraments. The emergence of Bible societies, and organizations like the Gideons, reflects to some extent the assumption that the Bible communicates directly to individuals without the mediation of the Church. Without any church or preacher, someone alone on a desert island (or at least in a hotel room) can read the Bible and become a Christian. Many see the central focus of Christian mission not as fostering worship or the growth of Christian communities, but simply as the propagation of the Bible.

As society in some countries became increasingly secular, and people's ties with the traditions of the Church were loosened, this concept of the Bible as a free-standing authority developed to extremes. People like Jehovah's Witnesses and others assume that since the Bible is an authoritative divine revelation we can read it "from scratch" simply to find out for ourselves the information it contains, without reference at all to the traditional Christian faith. This results virtually in a new religion, quite different from what Christians have always believed. In particular, the subtle Christian perception of the relationship between the Old Testament and the New Testament disappears: the Bible is just the Bible, one text just as important as any other. Others have found hidden codes in the Bible, implanted by some extra-terrestrial being to await the development of modern computer technology before anyone could understand them.

And so the Bible has been set free from its enslavement to the established Church authorities, only to face the dangers that always come with freedom. It is now not necessarily connected with the Church at all, but at the mercy of anyone who cares to read it – Christian or non-Christian, educated or ignorant, traditional or unconventional, dull or imaginative, or just plain potty! It is read by people who have no perception of its origins or its historic function within the Christian faith, but simply see it as some kind of supernatural revelation from heaven imparting information about God, heaven, the future, or whatever else one wishes to know.

Most of us do not go to such extremes as this, but we are all to some extent influenced by the idea that the Bible is an entity in itself, standing over against the Church, and to which the Church must be obedient. In thinking this, we have probably gone further than the Reformers, particularly Luther, ever intended. For them, the Bible was not something totally separate from the Church. It was superior to the current traditions because it was close to the origins, to those special events through which God had revealed himself and brought salvation to the world. They understood quite clearly that the writers of the Bible – the prophets, apostles and so on – were part of the community of faith just like ourselves. The difference was that they were much nearer than we are to the source of the revelation, and they were inspired by God to give a true account of it. We must therefore, they said, be guided by them. In that sense the Bible was an authority *within* the church. It was not something totally separate from "tradition", but simply the oldest and most authentic *part* of "tradition". The writers of the Bible are all in effect saying to us, in the words of Paul, "I received from the Lord what I also handed on to you" (1 Cor.11:23) – in other words, they are the purveyors of *tradition*.

### The Bible or Culture?

All these changes in perception of the Bible raise the question of what its "authority" means in practice. In the days when all Western Christendom assumed that the Roman Catholic Church was the sole authoritative interpreter of scripture, it was in practice the Church, not scripture that was the authority. The Church's interpretation, in turn, was worked out in practice by Catholic scholars. But they, like all scholars, were educated according to the assumptions of their time. In the Middle Ages, these assumptions were still those of ancient Greco-Roman civilization. The pillars of truth were thought to be scripture, tradition and reason, but "reason" in practice was Aristotelian philosophy. And so the Bible was still understood in ways that owed more to secular philosophy than to the Bible itself.

Whenever churches or individuals maintain that their sole authority is scripture, there is inevitably an element of self-deceit about it. The authority is not just scripture itself, but ideas from outside scripture which condition the way scripture is read. The

Reformers' assertion that scripture should be understood not allegorically but in its "plain meaning" was a refreshing and revolutionary idea at the time, but it is by no means as simple as it sounds. What is the "plain meaning"? Obviously, we answer, the meaning as understood by any normal person with common sense. But what is the difference between Protestant "common sense" and Catholic "reason"? Both are equally influenced by the prevailing philosophy of the time.

We cannot avoid bringing some presupposition, some unquestioned assumption, to our reading of the Bible. These presuppositions come from a wider context, the social and cultural environment. We see this being worked out in some of the new forms of church life that appeared with the Reformation. Luther simply wanted to reform some of the abuses in the Church: he was generally content with its traditional shape. Calvin and others, however, had more radical ideas. There soon emerged the Presbyterian pattern of church government, in which instead of the self-appointing succession of bishops there were elected elders, councils and synods. This was an order built on the concepts of democratic election, mutual supervision and accountability. Then came the congregational pattern adopted by Independents, Baptists and others, by which every local congregation was seen as a church in itself, directly under the guidance of the Holy Spirit with no need of any higher human authority.

These different patterns were passionately advocated on the basis of scripture. However, with some historical hindsight we can see today that the new church patterns emerging at that time were part of a general change taking place in society. The rise of the trading middle classes was challenging the old feudal society and developing ideas of citizenship and participation. Scripture was being interpreted in the light of the "common sense" assumption that people had the right to a say in how their Church should be governed – actually a fairly new idea at the time. The Catholic rearguard was still wedded to the old feudal forms of society, and they too found their justification in scripture.

At first, all this argument about the proper order for the Church had behind it the unquestioned assumption that the Church and the State were two sides of the same coin. Ever since the Roman emperor Constantine had called the Council of Nicaea to sort out some doctrinal problems, it had been assumed that a Christian ruler was responsible for upholding the true faith in his realm. The Reformation at first made no difference to this assumption. Luther's way of ordering church life spread from one German principality to another as each prince was persuaded to adopt it. Calvin worked with the burghers of Geneva to reform religion in that city. In Scotland, the establishment of Presbyterianism was a matter of the people's victory over the will of a Catholic monarch. In sixteenth-century England, the pattern of religious orthodoxy changed from one reign to another, with an enormous amount of blood shed by martyrs on both sides. None of these rulers, whichever side they were on, had any doubt that the regulation of the people's faith and worship was their responsibility. We still have a watered-down version of this in most European countries today. In England the government still appoints bishops and the monarch has the title "Defender of the Faith", while in Germany Christian ministers are paid by the State out of the "church tax".

It was the Anabaptists of the early sixteenth century who first challenged this assumption. They were followed later by the Separatists, Independents, Quakers and others. These people asserted that faith is a matter between God and the individual, and no civil authority has the right to control people's religious beliefs. This is something we take for granted in Western culture today, but at that time it was a novel and dangerous idea. A strong case could of course be made for it from the New Testament. Early Christianity was obviously a voluntary movement that had nothing to do with the State: but in the circumstances of that time what else could it be? As far as the sixteenth century is concerned, we have to question whether the emergence of this idea at that particular time came from the Bible or from contemporary movements in society. The emerging middle class of literate, articulate trades people who had begun to challenge the feudal system and the guilds would naturally begin to demand freedom of belief. In a sense, freedom of belief was the religious side of free trade.

The same could be said of the changes that have taken place in Christian ethics. For at least fifteen hundred years Christians assumed that the "usury" condemned in the Bible (Ex.22:25; Deut.23:19-20) meant lending money in order to make a profit. In the Middle Ages they often resorted to Jews, who had no scruples about charging interest to Christians: a situation reflected in Shakespeare's *The Merchant of Venice*. The capitalist society in which most of us live today could not function without the system of lending and borrowing with interest. Of course we disapprove of unscrupulous profiteering, but it hardly occurs to any Christian today that there is anything inherently wrong about using the money markets to maximize your investments. Even a church could find itself in legal trouble if it neglected to invest its funds profitably. The Christian U-turn on this issue took place mainly in the sixteenth century, and probably owed more to fifteenth-century Italian bankers than to biblical scholars!

We may yet see, if not another U-turn, at least a re-visiting of this issue. Many people today are questioning the whole system of capitalism because of the way it impoverishes so many people while making a minority rich, and the way it promotes the kind of unchecked growth that threatens the sustainability of life on this planet. People are experimenting with more co-operative and democratic ways of doing business. Banks are finding that more and more people are willing to invest in ethical funds, and quite happy with the results. Many Christians are involved in these developments and find support for them in the Bible. At the turn of the millennium the British churches led a campaign for the cancellation of the debts of poorer countries, and called it "Jubilee 2000", drawing on the biblical concept of the jubilee year in which debts had to be cancelled, bonded servants set free, and so on (Lev.25).

However, the main driving force for change still comes from secular political thinking that is not specifically Christian. The day may yet come when the churches and most Christians will see capitalism as un-Christian and un-biblical. However, this too would be the result not of pure unbiased Bible study but mainly of pressures from outside the church. Part of that pressure could even come from Muslims, who have consistently banned usury. In some Western countries Muslims are setting up banks and finance houses that operate in a way compliant with Islamic principles, and are beginning to attract attention and approval from people who are not of their faith.

Similarly, the idea that slavery is inherently wrong is a comparatively modern one. When attempts were made to abolish it, it was the opponents who based their arguments on the Bible. There could be nothing wrong with slavery, they said, because the Bible sanctioned it as part of the order of human society. The Hebrew scriptures specifically allow people, within certain regulations, to acquire slaves (Lev.25:44-46). To abolish slavery would, according to them, undermine the divinely ordained order of things: it was as "biblical" to those people as "family values" are to many people today. William Wilberforce and his associates in the campaign for abolition were evangelical Christians for whom the Bible was of supreme importance, but it is significant that their arguments were based on the central teachings of Jesus about love for one's neighbor, and took little notice of the Bible passages that specifically deal with slavery. It was the slave owners who were more interested in those passages. Once again, there has been a huge change in ethical attitudes, which, in spite of the prominent part taken in it by evangelical Christians, may well owe at least as much to eighteenth century secular ideals of humanity as it does to the content of the Bible as such.

In our own day, the same kind of thing is happening with the equality of the sexes. Feminist writers have quite rightly pointed out that the Bible is not as exclusively patriarchal as its male inter-preters have usually assumed it to be. However, we cannot hide from the fact that the biblical culture in general was one in which it was assumed that men were in charge and women took second place. Once again, society is moving on and Christians, like other people but perhaps a bit more slowly, are changing their attitudes. This is not happening through people just noting what the Bible says. It is happening through the challenge of the present day situation. In so far as people turn to the Bible on this issue, they are turning to it with a purpose: to find a biblical basis for inclusiveness and equality. It is not so much a case of the Bible changing contemporary culture as of culture changing the way we read the Bible.

More conservative believers see all this as a loss of conviction, a selling out to the values of "the world", following the fashion of the moment instead of the word of God. There are two answers to this charge. One is that it is nothing new: as we have seen, it has always happened. The other is that those of us who hold these "modern" beliefs about equality and so on are not usually motivated by a mere desire to follow fashion: we see them as fundamentally Christian principles. There is a movement going on that is similar to the Reformation, in fact a kind of continuation of it, trying to cut away the rank growth of traditions and go back to the roots of Christianity as it was meant to be. Part of this "new Reformation" is that it looks back not to the Bible as a monolithic, consistent authority, but to what seem to be the spiritual high points of the Bible, and supremely the inspiration of Jesus. However, this cannot be a one-way road: there is an inevitable dialogue between contemporary culture and the Bible that has to be honestly accepted.

The question "where is the real authority?" has thus been an issue throughout Christian history. Even with the most valiant attempts to hold to "scripture alone", we are confronted in the Bible with a huge, complex set of writings, and we can only make sense of them by adopting a particular perspective. In some ways the material contained in the Bible is rather like the stars in the sky. We see the "constellations" we have been taught to see, the pictures of mythical characters seen in the sky by the ancient Babylonians and Greeks. In spite of the modern discoveries of astronomy, we still cannot banish those patterns from our minds: indeed, astronomers still use them as a basic mapping system, while at the same time making other models and images to which the constellations are irrelevant.

We human beings find it very hard – perhaps impossible – to grasp anything without having a pattern: a "model" as scientists often call it. The same is true of the Bible. This vast, rather untidy collection of material has to be organized in some way. In order to grasp it we must read it in the light of some unifying principle around which everything else falls into place. Those who have different unifying principles end up virtually reading a different Bible. The particular "slant" we bring to our reading of the Bible shows itself in the verses we underline, in the passages we tend to read most frequently, or in the texts most often quoted in our tradition.

Those in the Catholic tradition see the Bible as part of the revelation of God's truth, first in creation, then in the Old Testament, then supremely in Christ, then in the Apostles to whom Christ entrusted it, and now in the Church, which is the sacrament of Christ's presence in the world. Within this revelation is redemption, the forgiveness of fallen human beings through the death and resurrection of Christ, but the benefits of this are administered primarily through the priesthood and the sacraments of the Church. The Catholic sees the Bible as the authoritative Word of God within this framework.

For Protestant evangelicals, as for Catholics, the forgiveness of sins through the cross and resurrection is the heart of the matter, but they focus it more personally, and see it as a direct relationship with Christ that does not depend on the Church. Individual believers are sustained in their faith by scripture and prayer and the fellowship of the Church, but not primarily through the mediation of the Church's priesthood. For the evangelical, the Bible is the inspired teaching of this message of personal salvation.

For many modern believers, the focus is different again. They see in the Bible humanity's developing understanding of the true nature of God, the supremacy of love, and the ever-living hope that God's kingdom of justice and peace will come on earth. For them, the cross of Christ is the central symbol of God's victory through suffering.

All these basic patterns of belief can find support in the Bible, but they lead to different ways of reading it, resulting in the Bible taking on different shapes. The re-shaping of the Jewish scriptures to form the Christian Old Testament is just one early example of this. This, however, must mean that the guide we are following is never purely the Bible itself, but whatever we perceive to be the unifying principle. Throughout Christian history, the supreme authority of the Bible on matters of theology, ethics and church order has never been as real as Christians thought it to be. The theologians have always read into the Bible the kind of things people of their time and culture wanted to hear, or perhaps the only things that, within their culture, they *could* hear.

This is not by any means to say that the Bible has not deeply influenced the Church and Christian culture. There is always a two-way process, a dialogue between the contemporary culture and the biblical message. People have been challenged by things they have read in the Bible, but this is a very different thing from the Bible being *in reality* the supreme authority. Ironically, when a faith community makes a book its supreme authority, it is usually in practice the community itself that ends up being the authority.

# 6. VOICES FROM ANOTHER WORLD?

The past few centuries have seen a profound change in the way we see everything, including the Bible. Scientific discoveries and new ways of thinking have for most people knocked the authoritative Bible off its pedestal and engendered a whole new attitude to authority in general. A huge change in human thought began with the Renaissance and came to a peak in the eighteenth century "Enlightenment": the movement away from mythology to rational, scientific thinking. Building on the Renaissance practice of observing and experimenting rather than just accepting ancient authorities, people began to discover universal natural laws by which the world seems to work. Miracles, and even God, began to appear redundant. For the first time, atheism and agnosticism became respectable options. Everything was open to doubt.

This had a particularly devastating effect on people's view of the Bible. The Reformation emphasis on the "plain meaning" actually intensified the problem. By the eighteenth century the old way of "explaining" difficult passages allegorically was hardly an option. The Bible was assumed to be a divine revelation making plain statements that anyone with common sense could understand. People assumed that what it said about history, astronomy, geology, botany or any other subject it touched upon was a simple, accurate statement of fact. This made it all the more difficult to maintain faith in the Bible when scientific research started to show that many of its statements, taken in their "plain meaning", were simply not true.

We tend to think of the publication of Darwin's *Origin of Species* in 1859 as the "crunch" moment in this process. However, long before this, scholars concerned with the Bible itself had begun to cast doubt on its accuracy. Before the end of the eighteenth century, rationalist scholars had begun to study the Bible as they would study any other piece of ancient literature. The traditional view of the authorship of certain books was being questioned on grounds of style and content. People were suggesting that Moses did not write the five books attributed to him, that David wrote few if any of the Psalms, and that the writings attributed to Solomon came from a much later age and different culture. Doubt was being cast on some of the letters in the New Testament that claim to be written by Paul.

Much of this was not new. Disputes about the authorship of some of the biblical writings have existed through most of Christian history. People like Erasmus in the sixteenth century were reviving questions that had occupied Jerome more than a thousand years before and had never been completely silenced. By the early nineteenth century, however, there was emerging a much more critical study of some of the hitherto unquestioned writings. People were beginning to comb through the Gospels in quest of the "historical Jesus". Instead of taking the Gospels as straightforward accounts of Jesus, they were looking at them, as it were, with a detective's eye: trying to see the way they were put together, the circumstances and motives of those who wrote them, and reading between the lines to deduce who Jesus really was, what he taught and what actually happened to him.

There was also the study of anthropology and human culture, stimulated by world exploration and the growth of the European empires. Scholars were finding parallels in Middle Eastern culture and elsewhere that cast light on the original meaning of some of the customs and stories found in the Hebrew scriptures. On the basis of these they were suggesting that the meaning of some stories and practices was something different from the meaning the scriptures give to them. And so, by the time the theory of evolution was cast onto an unsuspecting world by Darwin, scholars whose work was focused on the Bible itself had already been beavering away to undermine its authority as traditionally understood.

## The "Culture Gap"

It is important to realize that none of us has escaped the impact of modern ways of thinking about the Bible. Many have resisted it, but no-one has escaped it. Those who now hold a fundamentalist, or conservative, view of the authority of scripture hold it self-consciously and defensively. In the eighteenth century most people viewed the Bible as an infallible authority because they were not aware that there was any other way to view it. Today those who believe this are fully aware that there are other points of view, and that their view is a "position" to which they are committed and which they have to justify and defend. None of us can now read the Bible with the innocence of earlier generations, simply accepting it without question.

Moreover, it is hard for us now to enter into the minds of people of earlier centuries and grasp how they *really* viewed the Bible and their own faith. It is probably anachronistic even to say that they believed the Bible literally. They often, as we have seen, saw a difference between a literal and an allegorical meaning, but they probably did not quite draw the distinctions we do between "literal" and "symbolic" or "poetic". The way in which we tease out the difference between these ways of interpreting something is itself a product of the modern scientific mentality. People today, for instance, who question whether or not the resurrection of Jesus was a literal resuscitation of his body may say that they believe in the resurrection in the same way as the first Christians believed in it. However, this can never be proved or disproved, because we cannot travel back two thousand years in time and get inside the mind of the first Christians. In any case, no-one living in Western culture today can believe anything *exactly* in the same way as someone living in the first century.

The "modernist" or "liberal" view of the Bible today is not, as fundamentalists would argue, a clean break with an unbroken tradition of faith. It is just another stage in the process of change that has always been going on. Nor is the fundamentalist view of scripture a faithful perpetuation of what Christians have always believed. It is a specific response to a specifically modern problem. The way in which present-day conservative evangelicals express their faith is not purely the New Testament way. It is the product of centuries of history and tradition. A time-traveler from the early days of Christianity would find the twenty-first century's "evangelicalism" just as strange as its "liberalism".

This raises the whole question of the "culture gap" between our world and that of the Bible. No-one now believes that the Bible came floating down out of the heavenly world into ours. However, we are more aware than ever that it comes to us from a different world here on this planet, a world separated from us by two thousand years. The Bible still speaks to us across the centuries, alongside the voice of our church, our culture and our individual spiritual experience. But how can we hear what it has to say to us? What sense do we make of it?

It is in many ways an alien book. If we are to make any sense of it today, we have to acknowledge this. We approach it across a "culture gap". This gap has widened even in the lifetime of many of us today, as more and more people live in big cities miles away from the countryside. Images like the shepherd and the sower have become more remote. Society today is organized in a different way. What does it mean to talk about "the kingdom of God" in a world where kings and queens are a rarity and democracy is regarded as the ideal form of government? What does the "word of God" mean in a culture in which people are encouraged to think for themselves, and new ideas are presented as points for discussion rather than decrees to be obeyed? How can we talk about "commandments" in a society that only under-stands "values"?

The world today has developed a sense of *relativity* that was rare in previous ages. Change is so rapid that even a schoolchild is fully aware that the world is not the same for this generation as it was for the last, nor will it be the same for the next. We have become aware that not only styles of clothing and architecture, but also ways of behavior, moral values, and the whole way we think changes from one generation to another and from one culture to another. Migration is creating a world in which more and more of us have to come to terms with the fact that our culture is not the only one. This creates tension, passionate opposition and often violence between one culture and another and between one religion and another. At the same time, it is teaching many people the lesson that beliefs are to a great extent the product of culture, which itself is shaped by the accidents of history. Many people today are aware that if they had been born in a different country, or even into a different family, they would probably have a quite different set of beliefs and values.

There is still a lot of very fierce and often vicious argument about religion. However, in many parts of the world, especially those that have embraced liberal democracy, the attitude has moved a long way towards tolerance. The recognition of different faiths, and the need to respect them, is built into our laws and educational system. Even the most committed of believers do not generally want to bring back a world in which everyone is compelled to have the same religion. The mainstream leaders of the great world faiths do not believe in deporting people or condemning them to death simply for preaching a different faith: a few hundred years ago in Christendom, this was normal.

It is interesting to observe the change in the terms we use to describe different types of Christianity. At one time they were called "persuasions": people were persuaded of the rightness of a point of view, and tried in turn to persuade others. Then they became "denominations": different labels for the different departments of one Church. Today the favored expression is "traditions". My family, and/or my nation and culture may have made me a Christian: specifically, a Protestant, or to be even more specific, a Baptist. I may be convinced of the rightness of this theological position, but that does not alter the fact that if I had been born into a different environment I could easily have been a Catholic, a Hindu or a Muslim. My particular faith is not something I worked out for myself from scratch: the most I can say is that it was my good fortune to be born into it! In fact, I am often not even sure about that, because I have an uneasy relationship with many of my fellow-Baptists. I disagree with some things they say, and there are traditional ways and attitudes I would like to see changed. Many of my friends in the Catholic tradition, or in other faiths, have this kind of critical relationship with their heritage too. At the same time, we realize that we cannot simply wipe out our tradition and start working everything out from first principles. We can only start seeking the truth from where we are.

This sense of cultural relativity is one of a number of features of today's world that make it very different from the world of the Bible. How are we to deal with this "culture gap"? Many people stress that translation of the Bible needs to be not just linguistic but cultural, that is, translation from one thought pattern into another. This attempt is sometimes made on the assumption that the Bible has only one meaning. Sometimes there lurks behind it an element of unconscious fundamentalism: an assumption that what the Bible says is the absolute truth, but disguised in the thought-forms of a different culture. We only need to "translate" it into our thought-forms and it will be the truth for us today. This, however, can lead to a kind of reductionism that ends up making the Bible redundant.

It has been suggested that Bultmann, the New Testament scholar mostly associated with this approach, tended to identify the message of the New Testament so completely with twentieth century existentialism that one had to ask: if we find existentialism a perfectly satisfactory way to explain our universe, why do we need the Bible to tell us what we know already? "Cultural translation" in this wholesale way raises the same kind of problems we saw while discussing the way the Bible has been seen as an authority. What "message" does the Bible have for us if we interpret it purely in terms of our own philosophy? Somehow there has to be a cutting edge, a kind of tension between the Bible and ourselves. It may be that we need to recognize and maintain the culture gap rather than try to bridge it too completely for the sake of "relevance" or "understanding". If we can let go of this implicit fundamentalism – the idea that the Bible has "a message", that is to say, one message for us – then we can begin to have quite a different and more exciting relationship with it. Rather than struggling hard to ascertain what its "real" message is, and then to express it "correctly" in terms of our own culture, we can learn to read the Bible *as it is* and let it speak to us as it may.

In a way, reading the Bible is like traveling in a foreign country. This can be difficult and uncomfortable: a language we cannot understand, customs that are unfamiliar, attitudes that seem strange to us. And yet if we are willing to expose ourselves to the experience, to make the effort to meet people, to watch and listen without jumping to instant judgment, to participate in the culture even if we feel a bit nervous about it, to make some attempt to learn the language, it can be enormously profitable as well as being great fun. It can mean that, if only for a short time, we have entered into another way of seeing the world, and can return home with new insights into our own culture too.

On one level, the cultural difference between our world and that of the Bible is a problem. There is the constant danger of misunderstanding the Bible. We have to learn something of the historical background if it is to be accessible to us. But on the other hand it is also an advantage. It draws us into dialogue, helps us to question some of our own assumptions, and challenges us to think about some of the deepest questions of human existence. As with people and cultures, so with the Bible, there is no real interaction unless we recognize that the other is actually different from ourselves. We then open ourselves to hear something new, and possibly even to change our minds.

Like any foreign culture, the Bible is not *entirely* alien. One of the joys of travel is those moments when we find that other people, no matter how different their language and culture, basically "tick" the way we do. The same is true of the Bible. It brings us stories in which the lapse of time seems not to matter, because some things about the world and human nature have never changed. There are characters we can identify with, situations we can recognize.

It is familiar, too, because of the continuity of history. No culture lives in a state of complete isolation. In the past two hundred years there has been so much change that we tend to think we live in a totally different world from that of past ages. There is undoubtedly a "culture gap", but we must beware of making it absolute. The gap between our culture and that of the Bible is not a gaping, empty chasm. It is an unbroken chain of generations, each of which has experienced some change in its view of the world. The change in recent generations has been immense, but we are still not entirely incapable of understanding the past and to some extent incorporating it into our perception of the world. The Bible, down through the ages, has been so much a part of the consciousness of every generation in Christendom that we can never say it is *completely* alien to the modern world. Our world is still to some extent shaped by it.

## Let the Bible be Itself

When we visit a foreign country we do not usually spend the time constantly working out how we can apply some of the lessons we are learning there when we get back home, or trying to decide whether these foreign ways are "right" or "wrong". We simply live there and go along with the experience. It is possible to do this with the Bible. We do not need to be constantly working out what it means and coming to conclusions: we can simply go along with the experience, and let it speak to us how it will. We can expose ourselves to the Bible and let it be itself.

One simple practical step in this direction might be to take much more care about the reading of the Bible in public worship. So often it is read poorly and incoherently, not only by inexperienced lay people but often by clergy too! Even when read clearly, it is often read in a sonorous tone that robs it of all expression, giving the impression of a ritual being observed rather than of any real communication. Every Bible passage belongs to a particular genre, and this surely needs to be observed when reading it. A psalm of praise, if it is not sung, should at least be read with a feeling of joy and celebration. A psalm of lamentation needs to be read in a way that will help us feel the sadness, maybe the desperation that first produced it. Some of the angry utterances of the prophets need to be read angrily, so that we feel something of their rage. Some of the stories in the Bible are entertaining, sometimes with touches of humor, and should be read accordingly. A miracle story (whatever doubts we may have about it in our minds) should make the congregation want to say "Wow!", or at least "Well, fancy that!"

Churches differ in their custom concerning what is said at the end of a Bible reading. "This is the word of the Lord" tends to be the favorite ending these days, but this raises problems. As we shall see later, there are serious questions to be asked about calling the Bible the word of God: the Bible nowhere calls itself by that title. Even for those who do believe it is the word of God, it is often unhelpful to give the impression that any given passage can be taken directly as God's authoritative word in any given situation. I once heard a preacher read the first chapter of Esther, the story of how king Xerxes' wife Vashti incurred his wrath by refusing to come to him when called. The king banished her from his presence for ever, and had this decision proclaimed throughout the land in order to ensure that all women would learn to obey their husbands. The preacher's comment was, "This is not the word of the Lord: it is the word of a drunken despot who didn't get his way"!

If you pressed people to say what they mean by "This is the word of the Lord", they might say something like this: "Taken in context, interpreted by sound hermeneutic principles in the light of Christian theology, under the guidance of the Holy Spirit, etc., etc., this Bible passage is truly part of God's word". It is difficult to explain all this to a congregation every time the Bible is read: would it not therefore make more sense not to say it? Jesus did not end his own parables by saying "This is the word of the Lord" – he usually said "Let anyone with ears to hear listen". In practice it could be more effective to end a Bible reading with a few seconds of silence, showing respect for the text and at the same time allowing people to react to it in whatever way it moves them.

Whether we are expounding the Bible in sermons or studying it privately, we need to shake off the habit of always bringing to it the baggage of what we have been taught to believe, or of what we think we already know. We need to use our imagination, based on our real experience of life. Some of the interpretations produced by such groups as the base communities in South America are disturbing to orthodox beliefs because they come to the Bible from the background not of academic theology or church history, but simply of their own experience. The parable of the wicked vineyard tenants for instance (Matt.21:33-41) looks different if you are working the land of a rich absent landlord and getting very little return for your labor! That other vineyard story, about the man who paid all his workers the same whether they had worked all day or just an hour (Matt.20:1-16) raises interesting questions when people who know what it is to queue up for casual labor start thinking about the justice of it instead of "spiritualizing" it as traditional European preachers do.

We need also to respect the integrity, the wholeness, of the Bible. Lectionaries often divide the Bible up into very small bite-sized chunks, and carefully omit passages that are tedious or "difficult". People who profess to have a "high" view of scripture are surely denying their own faith when they do this: if the Bible is the word of God, who are we to edit it? Who are we to imply that God really should not have said exactly those things in exactly that way? But even if we see the Bible as a fallible human work, we surely owe it the respect of taking it *as it is*. Sometimes we miss the point of a passage if we do not see it in its context as part of a chapter or even of the whole book. We can equally miss the point if we quietly ignore a bit that doesn't seem to fit in, or that grates on our spiritual sensitivity. These things were said in this particular way for a reason. We may not agree with them or like them, but it is dishonest to pretend they are not there, or that they "really" mean something else.

To take one example: in 2 Samuel 5 we find the story of David being made king and then going on to conquer Jerusalem and make it his capital. This is of course an important turning point, the beginning of the process by which Jerusalem became "the holy city", with all the associations and symbolism that has surrounded it for Jews and Christians. As such it well deserves a place in a lectionary. However, a lectionary recently produced prescribed the reading of verses 1-5 and 9-10. By selecting in this way, it missed out a rather obscure and unsavory passage involving the Jebusites' taunt that even the blind and the lame could hold David back from the city, and David's command to slaughter the blind and the lame as his enemies. This is followed by a comment that makes David's command a justification for the ban on blind and lame people in the sanctuary. Certainly this is a difficult and "unedifying" passage, but what is the effect of omitting it from the reading? What we are left with is a fairly simple statement that David conquered Jerusalem and reigned there. What we are allowed to forget is that military conquest, even in a religious cause, involves brutality and unscrupulous slaughter, and often leads on to discrimination against minorities. The Bible at this point *tells it as it is*. Whatever the thoughts of the original writer, reading it today challenges us to stop and think about the "underside" of all our religious pretensions, and especially to be wary of the naïve triumphalism that is often a feature of Christian "mission". As with life itself, so with the Bible, we often learn most from the hardest bits.

In sermons or in Bible study groups, we should perhaps not be asking what the passage teaches, as if we were studying a text book, but rather questions like: What made that person say this at that time? What motivated someone to recall it and write it down? What do we feel now as we read it? We should aim not so much to analyze a passage as to explore it and perhaps dramatize it. The experience of reading the Bible can in some ways be like that of watching a play or a film. We enter into the passion and the drama without making immediate moral judgments, and so, imperceptibly, we allow it to deepen our understanding, challenge our thinking, and in the long run help us grow as persons.

## Just a Drama?

The objection to treating the Bible in this way is that it might take the edge off the challenge of the gospel. Attending church, or taking part in Bible study, is not after all quite the same thing as going to the theatre. Preaching, many Christians say, is not just entertainment or intellectual stimulation: it is the declaring of truth. It calls for a verdict that will change the listener's life and make a difference to the world. It is not enough just to look at the Bible and make observations about it, or just to "enjoy" it as a work of art: there must be a real personal response. The idea of "the Bible designed to be read as literature" (the actual title of a book that was once popular) has been criticized on the ground that the Bible was never meant to be read "as literature". As the writer of John's Gospel puts it: "these (things) are written so that you may come to believe that Jesus is the Messiah, and that through believing you may have life in his name" (John 20:31).

In this book we have been noting numerous ways in which the Bible has been misused. If we read the Bible merely as entertaining or stimulating literature, are we not still misusing it?

This objection can be partly met by considering in what sense that passage in John's Gospel means "believe". "These things are written so that you may believe", certainly, but that is not simply a matter of believing "these things". The things said in the Bible are meant to help us believe in God through Jesus Christ. In other words, they are meant to lead us on beyond the things themselves to the God who is behind them. And surely a first, vital step towards this is to get inside the experience of the people who said them. We will then be in a better position to move beyond what they say to the God they experienced, and then, in our own words and ways, to express our experience of God meeting with us.

This is the real personal response to which the nature of the Christian faith calls us. It can never be a response of mere acceptance and obedience. We honor the Bible writers best by really listening to them and entering into their concerns and passions rather than by taking their words as timeless oracles. Obedience is due only to God, and we do not find out what God wants us to do by just accepting what the writers of the Bible said. They are witnessing to their experience of God and expressing it in their terms. Our listening to them, and being moved by what they say, is not the end of the matter: it is just one step in our own pilgrimage towards discovering what God has to say to *us*.

There are two different ways of learning. Some learning is a matter of receiving knowledge from authorities. This is necessary and normal in the early stages of learning any subject. We always need at least *some* "input" of information. No matter how brilliant you may be at interpreting history, you need at least to know the outline of what happened and when, and the quickest and easiest way to acquire this knowledge is from a standard text book or a teacher.

However, we also know that the deepest and most useful lessons in life are learned in a different way. We learn to understand people by entering into their experience. In the field of counseling, the expression often used is "creative listening". We go along with what another person is experiencing and feeling. We laugh with them and cry with them. This does not mean that we are entirely swallowed up by their feelings. We are still ourselves, and we retain some measure of objectivity. We may not agree with the other person's *interpretation* of their experience, but we recognize the *reality* of their experience and of their *perception* of it. By this approach we not only give another person the help and support they need, we learn at the same time something more about life and about ourselves. If we can shake off our conception of the Bible as an "authority" and read it from this point of view, then we may well find that it works as a "word of God" on a much deeper level than that of mere information.

## Our Own Story

There is another vital difference for believers between reading the Bible and reading any other literature, or watching a play or film. Whether we are Jews or Christians, we have a special relationship with this particular set of writings. We are not just listening to any old story: this is *our* story. As we read it we are engaging with our own heritage, our own ancestors in faith, and we ourselves are part of the story.

For many people the message of the Bible is expressed in just one small statement: "God is love". On the basis of this we could say that much of the material in the Bible is superfluous at best and, at worst, irreconcilable with that belief. But no matter how much we may simplify our faith we can never avoid the fact that we are part of a history. Even if it can all be summed up as "God is love", love can never be just a bare, abstract principle. To love means to love a particular person in a particular situation. Nor is it a timeless thing, in the sense of time being irrelevant to it. Every loving relationship has its own "love story", its unique stock of shared memories. Those memories may include painful ones, times of misunderstanding, times when we "lost the plot", times when we separated or quarreled. But these are all part of the story and of the relationship..

Western civilization is deeply influenced by the Judaeo-Christian tradition, of which the Bible is the oldest and central written deposit. Even for those who are not believers, the image of the God they do not believe in is shaped by that tradition! Not only for active Christians, but for all who have some residual Christian faith, the Bible is the culture, the thought-world in which their faith is largely expressed and lived. Sometimes it is said that Christians of different traditions can find their unity in the Bible. As we have seen, this is misleading if we mean that all our disagreements would dissolve if only we all stuck to the Bible's instructions. However, in another sense – what we might call a cultural sense – it is perfectly true that we are united by the Bible. All Christian churches have lived and grown with the Bible as their constant companion, a background and stimulus to all their thinking. Christians of all kinds have interpreted their lives within the framework of the Bible stories. The Bible's images are a common language in which Christians talk with each other. We call God King, Lord or Father – though some of us may now question these masculine images. We talk of the problems of the world in terms of sin, atonement, reconciliation and redemption. We express our hopes and ideals as "the kingdom of heaven" or "the new Jerusalem". The style of the Psalms has become the style of Christian prayer and praise. When we reflect on human charac-teristics, problems and situations in the light of our faith, we almost instinctively turn to the characters and stories of the Bible as models to help us understand them. Like all languages, that of Christians has changed through the centuries, but the Bible is still the bedrock of its heritage.

It is true that there is a reaction today against the way in which some pious Christians are unable to communicate with the ordinary world because they are so steeped in "the language of Canaan". Ironically, that expression itself falls into its own category – in order to understand it, you have to read Isaiah 19:18! It is also true that in our present secular and multi-cultural society the Christian faith has to be talked about in language that is generally understood, and this may not be biblical language. However, communicating the message in a post-Christian culture usually means not an abandoning of the Bible but simply a more creative and imaginative use of it. Educationalists were once advocating a move away from biblical material in the teaching of the Christian faith to children, but this is now in many quarters felt to have been mistaken. What was wrong in the traditional way of teaching was not the use of Bible stories as such, but just the way in which the Bible was presented as sacrosanct and not open to question.

As we free ourselves from a false kind of deference to biblical authority, we find new life, meaning and usefulness in many of the Bible stories and themes. We have only to think of shows and films like *Jesus Christ Superstar*, *The Last Temptation of Christ*, *Jesus of Montreal*, *Corpus Christi*, *The Passion of the Christ*, or *Jerry Springer – the Opera*, to realize that creative artists today are as fascinated as ever by the stories and images of the Bible.

The Bible's "love story" is a developing one, but the development is not straightforward. The saying "the course of true love never runs smoothly" is especially applicable to the Bible! Some parts of the tradition are a direct expression of the best and highest conception of God, but more often than not this conception has been expressed in tension with the tradition, and sometimes in opposition to it. The supreme example of this for Christians is the fact that Jesus himself was condemned to death by those who were the tradition's chief representatives and defenders. The whole Judaeo-Christian history is a tale of challenge, conflict, development and sometimes complete transformation. Nevertheless, the story of God's love affair with humanity, as Christians see it and tell it, is bound up inseparably with that stream of history that flows from Abraham, Isaac and Jacob through the Jewish nation into the Christian church of the present day. Without that story, and without the images and thought-forms of that culture, the love of God would be just a philosophical principle. With the Bible, it becomes a warm, living human story.

This is not to say that we must stick rigidly to the biblical images and refuse to draw on equally powerful and telling images from elsewhere. Some of the most profound insights into the meaning of life and the nature of God have emerged in other stories too, in quite different cultures like Hinduism, Buddhism or ancient Chinese wisdom. We must not close our minds to this and think that Jews or Christians have a copyright on God! The fact that the same kind of message emerges elsewhere in human culture should in fact reinforce our faith. If people of a quite different culture have seen it too, this confirms our belief that there is some universal reality in it. Already within the Bible, the tradition related to other cultures and drew inspiration from them. The Hebrew scriptures are not simply an expression of ancient Hebrew belief and culture: they draw richly on Canaanite, Babylonian, Persian and Greek ideas. The New Testament reflects the cosmopolitan world in which it came into being. We easily recognize that John's Gospel with its talk of the Logos draws on the ideas of Greek philosophy and culture, but this is also true of Paul and the other New Testament writers.

Human cultures are constantly growing, changing and mingling with each other. However, if we are Christians at all we inevitably see the Bible story as being somehow the central plot in God's relationship with humanity. The Bible story, with all its ups and downs, all its byways, all its unfortunate developments, all its tensions, is still *our* story.

## The Ongoing Dialogue

As we have seen, the fixing of the boundaries of scripture was a result of controversy. It revolved very much around the question of who had the authentic, original gospel: do "they" have it, or do "we"? The church leaders of the time may have had a naïve view of tradition as something smooth and unbroken, passed on unchanged from the beginning, but in reality Christian theology has always been changing and developing, and at the same time always in dialogue with its past. In modern times we have come to realize that this dialogue can involve real disagreement. We do not have to accept what has been handed down and simply obey it: we can argue with it.

Sometimes some very important aspect of Christian faith may fade into the background, and something in the Bible can serve as a healthy reminder of it. Sometimes a whole generation can develop an unbalanced view that neglects some important biblical insight, and a renewal of Bible study can call it back to its senses. This was largely the point Karl Barth was making when he challenged early twentieth century liberalism and tried to recall the Protestant churches to a more truly biblical faith. It is also partly what lies behind the new emphasis on the Bible in Roman Catholicism since the Second Vatican Council. A return to the Bible can be a return to the fullness of Christian faith from a tradition that represented only part of it: a return to the roots, and a challenge to clear away the irrelevant undergrowth that has surrounded them.

In practice, however, those movements of renewal that have gone "back to the Bible" have been inspired by a particular *part* of the Bible. Luther's gospel of free grace was inspired by things he read in Paul's Letter to the Romans, not by the catalogue of rewards and punishments in the Book of Deuteronomy. The faith that fuelled the emancipation of slaves and the movement for civil rights for black people in America was inspired by the story of the Exodus, not by the approving references to slavery in other parts of the Bible. What we find when we go "back to the Bible" depends, quite rightly, on what we are looking for, or on what we need to hear. A return to the Bible, the whole Bible and nothing but the Bible is unlikely ever to produce renewal.

Nor is it always a matter of the Bible recalling us to its own themes and insights. There is a two-way movement. Certainly there are themes in the Bible that we do well to take seriously even if they are not in accord with the trend of our own time, but the converse is also true. The perception of Jesus and his meaning that we have because of our present-day experience includes insights that may not be in the Bible, or may be under-represented in the Bible. Today, for example, we see more clearly something that the Bible says at the very beginning and yet somehow seems to forget later, that men and women are equally made in the image of God. We also today have a clearer insight into the variety of human sexuality, and a deeper psychological understanding of people's behavior generally. There must therefore always be a dialogue between the Bible and ourselves.

However, helpful dialogue only comes about by listening. It is not achieved through politeness or pretending. We have to acknowledge that we are different, and see and hear each other as we are. And so, as far as reading and interpreting the Bible are concerned, the first vital step is to *let the Bible be itself*. Paradoxically, only by being itself, "warts and all", can it really have something to say to us.

# 7. THE BIBLE AND THE WORD OF GOD

The designation "word of God" for the Bible is not itself biblical. In the Hebrew scriptures "the word of God" usually means the message the inspired prophet receives from God and passes on. In the New Testament it usually refers to the message preached by the apostles. But supremely the "Word of God" is Jesus himself, described in the first chapter of John's Gospel as "the Word made flesh". We have no authority in the Bible itself for calling the Bible the word of God. All we have is the experience of many Christians that they find God speaking to them in the Bible. But, as we have seen, this in practice means in *parts* of the Bible.

## Is Fundamentalism Evangelical?

In the chief founder-figure of Protestantism, Martin Luther, we find a much more dynamic conception of the "word of God" than the dominant Protestant one that developed after his time. For Luther, it was not so much a visual experience as an aural one: not the words on the printed page, but the personal experience of being addressed by God. He read the Bible, as it were, not with his eyes to "look up" doctrinal information and ethical rules, but with his ears, to listen to God.

In our experience as human beings, words do not simply impart information: they often *do* something. They are a kind of transaction. They create, reinforce, maintain and sometimes break relationships. Just the word "hello" can create a relationship where there was not one before. The word "sorry" can stop an unpleasant incident from developing into a quarrel. The words "I love you" can sometimes change two lives for ever, and it only remains for the words "I do" to make it official! Words can cause offence and hurt people, or they can bring about reconciliation. The nickname you were given as a child, or the adjectives that were applied to you, can deeply affect you for the rest of your life. Our words can commit us to a course of action: "I give you my word" puts us in a situation from which it is difficult to withdraw. We may not believe as we used to in "magic words", but a word said at the right time by a powerful person can still do wonders! A whole career can sometimes be changed by someone "putting in a word" for us. For Luther, it was in this sense that "the word of God" could be found in the Bible. In it, the living God *does* something to us. He rebukes us, judges us, warns us, forgives us, encourages us, makes promises to us, changes us.

Luther's activity as a reformer grew out of an overwhelming experience of the grace of God in Christ. When all his prayers, pilgrimages and good works had failed to make him feel right with God, he had made the discovery that it is God himself who puts us right with himself by the sacrifice of Christ on the cross, and we grasp this salvation by simply believing. The movement Luther started was a campaign not primarily to get people reading the Bible, but to get them to realize free salvation in Christ. The slogan "scripture alone" is often quoted as a rallying-cry of the Reformation, but for Luther this was not the first principle: it was the third. First there was "grace alone": salvation is purely by the grace of God. Then there was "faith alone": all that is asked of us is faith. "Scripture alone" was necessary as a weapon against the opponents who condemned him on the grounds of tradition and ecclesiastical authority.

"Scripture alone" for Luther did not mean that we are bound to accept the whole of scripture as an infallible authority. For him, the gospel of free grace through Christ was paramount, and nothing in Church teaching, *or even in scripture*, must be allowed to obscure or hinder it. He believed that Christians must judge for themselves which scriptures "proclaim Christ", and honor them accordingly: not, as the church authorities did, obscure the simplicity of the gospel by insisting on the equal validity of all scripture. He himself had great doubts about some of the books in the New Testament. He even said once that he would like to burn the Epistle of James. However, his general conception of scripture was more subtle and dynamic than that. Rather than advocating that some books should be removed, he recognized that someone else might well hear the true gospel of Christ in places where he himself had been unable to hear it. The "word of God" was not in the printed words alone, but in the interaction between the words and the reader, under the inspiration of the Holy Spirit. Luther's main concern was that people should know the good news of free forgiveness in Christ, and then feed their faith on the Bible in so far as they found that good news in it.

Unfortunately Luther's insight was brushed aside by later developments. The sharp conflict between the Reformers and the Roman Catholic authorities led to an extreme polarization. The Roman Catholic Church, in the Council of Trent, asserted more positively than ever the authority of tradition *alongside* that of scripture, while the Protestants developed an ever higher and stricter doctrine of scripture as the sole and complete authority. This view of the Bible has in fact been destructive of the best insights of the Reformation. Having to obey the whole Bible is in the end just as damaging to the gospel of grace as having to obey a pope or a church. If the laws in Leviticus and Deuteronomy are to have equal validity with the Gospel of John or the Letter to the Romans, if Paul's restrictive views about women are just as authoritative as his preaching of salvation by grace, or if the detailed prescriptions about church order and discipline found in many parts of Paul's first Letter to the Corinthians are just as divinely inspired as the glorious hymn to love in chapter 13, then the gospel of the grace of Christ for which the Reformers stood is obscured beyond all recognition. We are back to a system of religious and moral rules, and those who claim to have understood the scriptures correctly are licensed to dominate others. This is why Protestant fundamentalism has often produced effects just as viciously oppressive as anything in mediaeval Roman Catholicism.

Fortunately, in spite of whole-Bible fundamentalism, something of this dynamic sense of the word of God still remains in Protestant evangelical piety. When people talk about a preacher "bringing us the word" they are thinking of the word of God not just as the printed words in the Bible but as the communication of the good news by a living human being. As concerned as they are to uphold their high doctrine of scripture, even some of the most conservative of evangelical Christians have not lost sight of their fundamental belief that a relationship with God through Jesus Christ is the heart of the matter.

This is revealed very interestingly in the day-to-day relationship most Christians have with the Bible. Probably uniquely among the religions of the world, many Christians, and especially those in the evangelical tradition, have a very casual attitude towards their scripture as a physical object. Jews treat the scrolls of the Torah with great reverence. They are hand-written on parchment, kept in a sacred place, and ceremonially paraded in worship. In a Sikh Gurdwara the Guru Granth is literally exalted: it is taboo to place oneself physically above it or on the same level. Muslims are offended by seeing a copy of the Qur'an in a bookshop anywhere except on the top shelf. However, for most Western Christians a copy of the Bible is just a book. For a long time Bibles were nearly always bound in black with gold page edging, but this is becoming much rarer. Now there are many different editions, some with brightly colored covers and the text inside broken up by little cartoons.

Having bought a Bible in a bookshop, Christians will only give it the usual care they give to any possession. They will not treat it with special reverence. They will cheerfully put it in a bag with the rest of their shopping, carry it around with them in a handbag, or slip it into a pocket. There is an edition of the Bible on punched sheets for insertion into a personal organizer. In fact, the very people who believe most firmly and earnestly in scripture are often the most casual in handling their own Bible. They underline certain passages and scribble comments in the margin. They use the covers as a receptacle for newspaper cuttings, sermon notes and all sorts of bits and pieces. It is the people who never actually *read* the Bible who tend to treat it as a sacred object. A Bible with frayed edges, loose pages and grubby finger marks is a positive sign of piety!

All this indicates that even for the most conservative of Christians it is not the book as such that is sacred, but the words in it. In fact even that is not quite true. Christians are probably unique among the world religions in their casual attitude to the original words of their scriptures. Jewish children are expected to learn Hebrew in order to read the Torah. For Muslims the Qur'an is the original Arabic and no translation into another language can actually be "the Qur'an". Some Muslims who are illiterate, or unable to understand Arabic, draw spiritual inspiration from simply *looking* at a page of the Qur'an in the belief that those marks they cannot understand are the very words of God. The majority of Christians, on the other hand, have very little concern about the original scripture. There are devout Christians who know the Bible from cover to cover in their own language but are not even aware that the Old Testament was written in Hebrew and the New Testament in Greek. Even trained clergy have not always learned these languages, and many who learned them would not think of using them in their personal reading of the Bible. They can even be heard *boasting* that they have forgotten whatever Greek or Hebrew they learned!

Now that many English-speaking Christians have broken free from their bondage to the King James Version, we find the Bible translated in all kinds of ways. We have the Street Bible, the Bible in Cockney rhyming slang, the Bible in the dialect of Liverpool or

Glasgow, the Bible in limerick verses, the Bible as a comic strip –
who knows what next? It seems that the main priority is not to
convey the exact wording of the original writings, but to make
sure that, somehow or other, people read the Bible and get the
message. Probably no other religion treats its original scriptures in
this cavalier way.

Part of the reason for this is historical. For most of the Middle
Ages Western Christendom virtually lost touch with the original
scriptures. The Latin translation – the Vulgate – became the
standard Bible. Western Christians in their anti-Semitism
despised the Hebrew language, and the separation of Rome from
the Eastern churches meant that Greek was associated with
heresy. The Vulgate became sacrosanct. Even after the
Reformation, when the Roman Catholic Church eventually
decided that it was permissible to translate the Bible into the
common tongue, the translations produced were not at first from
the original languages but from the Latin. This practice was
followed as recently as Ronald Knox's translation in the 1940s.
Though he paid attention to the Hebrew and Greek, his work was
basically a translation from the Latin.

The Reformers translated the Bible directly from the Hebrew
and Greek, but once they had made it available for ordinary
people to read they felt their job had been done. There was no
encouragement to the ordinary lay people to learn Hebrew or
Greek in order to read and judge for themselves. And so for
several centuries most people carried on using the first, or at least
a very early, translation that had been made into their language.
For English speaking people, this was the Authorized, or King
James, Version of 1611. This was never a theological principle, as
it had been with the Vulgate. There were always other translations available, and as far as the English-speaking world was
concerned the twentieth century saw a rich blossoming of new
translations, and a gradual ousting of the Authorized Version
from its exclusive status.

However, this peculiarly Christian attitude to scripture is not wholly explained by the accidents of history. It has a theological significance too. It reflects the basic nature of Christianity. For some other faiths the scripture is central in a way that it is not for Christianity. Jews define themselves as those who live by the Torah. For Muslims, the foundation of their religion is the revelation of the nature and will of Allah as found in the Qur'an. But Christians, however "high" their doctrine of scripture, are not primarily "people of the book". It is Jesus who is the foundation, and the heart of the Christian message is his crucifixion and resurrection. The place of the Bible is that it *witnesses* to these events. Conservative Christians believe it is an infallible witness, but for them too it is a witness rather than the reality itself.

### How does God speak?

The trouble with much thinking about the Bible is that it starts from the wrong end. Theologians have started from the statement that the Bible is the word of God, and then tried to work out what this should imply about it. Their unspoken assumption of what the "word of God" means has owed more to Greek philosophy than to the Bible itself. They have assumed that being the word of God it must be somehow pure and "ideal" in a Platonic sense, above all the imperfections of this world. It must be utterly consistent, it must be spiritually uplifting from cover to cover, and it must be without fault or inaccuracy of any kind. Having decided on philosophical grounds what the word of God should be, they then have enormous problems trying to fit the Bible, in all its mixed-up and messy reality, into this mold. It is worth considering how this would work if we looked at it from the other end. Why not say, "If the Bible is the word of God, what does it tell us about how God speaks"?

When we start looking at the actual content of the Bible, one of the most obvious features is that most of it is not written in the *form* of God speaking at all. Certainly in the commandments God

says "I am the LORD your God ...", and many of the teachings of
the prophets begin with: "Thus says the LORD ..." However, only
a small part of the Bible is in that form. Many parts, notably the
Psalms, are the other way around: they show people speaking to
God. Nor are they only praising God and saying good things
about him. They are often giving voice to their pain, their fear,
and their doubt. They are even reproaching God or arguing with
God. In many parts of the Bible people are talking to each other
*about* God. Large parts of the Bible consist of human stories, and
often in these stories God hardly comes into the picture at all. In
two books, Esther and the Song of Solomon, God is not even
mentioned.

Could this perhaps be telling us that the way God speaks is not
always, or even often, by direct oracles, but through all kinds of
voices? What we say *to* God, what we say *about* God, and the
things we do and say as we get on with the ordinary business of
life without even thinking of God, are all ways in which God
speaks. The Bible is obviously not "the word of God" in the sense
of a speech in which God addresses the world. It is a mixed
collection of stories, prayers and poems, a huge slice of human life
lived, sometimes consciously and sometimes unconsciously, in
the presence of God. And so, even if we call the Bible "the word
of God", its very form suggests that God speaks in many ways,
and only rarely in direct speech.

Again, the Bible is not a simple book that declares truth in a set
formula. It is not even always consistent with itself. The more we
read the Bible, the more we find that it plays with ideas, experi-
ments, develops them, turns them over to show them in a new
light, and sometimes actually rejects them. If we believe God
speaks through the Bible, this must surely imply that God too is
playful, experimental, changing and developing, even in some
mysterious way self-contradictory and self-correcting – in other
words, *alive*.

If we take the Bible seriously as a vehicle through which God speaks, we find there the kind of God who would be most unlikely to provide a final, definitive revelation of himself, and even less likely to do it in a book! The writers of the Bible themselves point us beyond the Bible to look for God. As one of the Psalms says: "The heavens are telling the glory of God... Day to day pours forth speech, and night to night declares knowledge..." (Ps.19:1-2). Jesus promised his disciples that the Holy Spirit would lead them into all truth (John 14:26; 16:13). The whole sweep of the Bible story through the Jewish community and the Christian Church is a constant reminder that the self-revealing of God did not cease at the moment when the last verse of the Bible was written. We ourselves are a vital part of the story. The Bible is a vital part of our story. But it is a part, not the whole.

# SUGGESTIONS FOR FURTHER READING

I give below a small selection from the huge literature that exists about the subjects and issues mentioned in this book. A few of the older books are now out of print, but are well worth reading if you can find them. Most of the really significant books have been reprinted and/or revised and this list gives, as far as I know, the latest editions.

James Barr, *The Bible in the Modern World*, SCM 1973

*Old and New in Interpretation: A Study of the Two Testaments*, SCM 1982

*Holy Scripture: Canon, Authority, Criticism*, Oxford University Press 2004

James Barr and John Barton, *The Scope and Authority of the Bible*, SCM 2002

John Barton, *People of the Book? The Authority of the Bible in Christianity*, SPCK 1993

*What is the Bible?* SPCK 1997

Christopher Evans, *Is 'Holy Scripture' Christian? And Other Questions*, SCM 1971

Gerd Lüdemann, *The Unholy in Holy Scripture: The Dark Side of the Bible*, tr. John Bowden, SCM 1997

Dennis Nineham, *The Use and Abuse of the Bible: A Study of the Bible in an Age of Rapid Social Change*, SPCK 1978

John Shelby Spong, *The Sins of Scripture: Exposing the Bible's Texts of Hate to Reveal the God of Love*, HarperCollins 2006

Keith Ward, *What the Bible Really Teaches: A Challenge for Fundamentalists*, SPCK 2004

N T Wright, *The Last Word: Scripture and the Authority of God, Getting Beyond the Bible Wars*, HarperOne 2006

For those who want to find out more about the history, I would recommend Lee Martin McDonald, *The Biblical Canon: Its Origin, Transmission and Authority*, Hendrickson 2007. This is a big book that covers most aspects of the history while still being readable for the non-specialist. Shorter and simpler accounts may be found in:

Karen Armstrong, *The Bible: The Biography*, Atlantic Books 2007
John Barton, *How the Bible Came to Be*, Westminster John Knox Press 1998
David D L Dungan, *Constantine's Bible: Politics and the Making of the New Testament*, SCM 2006 and Fortress 2007
Bart D Ehrman, *Lost Christianities: The Battles for Scripture and the Faiths we never knew*, Oxford University Press 2005
*Lost Scriptures: Books that did not make it into the New Testament*, Oxford University Press 2005
Harry Y Gamble, *The New Testament Canon: Its Making and Meaning*, Wipf & Stock 2002
Bruce M Metzger, *The Canon of the New Testament: Its Origin, Development and Significance*, Oxford University Press 1997
*The Oxford Illustrated History of the Bible*, ed. John Rogerson, Oxford University Press 2001
Jaroslav Pelikan, *Whose Bible is it? A History of the Scriptures through the Ages*, Penguin 2005

A good general reference book is Alec Gilmore, *A Concise Dictionary of Bible Origins and Interpretation*, T & T Clark 2007.

There are many useful guides, commentaries etc. for anyone wishing to read the Bible with the kind of approach suggested in this book. Here are a few of the best recent ones:

John Barton, *Reading the Old Testament: Method in Biblical Study*, Darton Longman and Todd 1996

Marcus Borg, *Reading the Bible Again for the First Time: Taking the Bible Seriously but not Literally*, HarperCollins 2002

Jack Good, *The Bible: Faith's Family Album*, Chalice 1999

James L Kugel, *How to Read the Bible: A Guide to Scripture then and now*, Free Press 2007 (covering only the Jewish Scriptures)

Roy Robinson, *The Thoughtful Guide to the Bible*, O Books 2004

# BOOKS

**O books**
O is a symbol of the world, of oneness and unity. In
different cultures it also means the "eye", symbolizing
knowledge and insight, and in Old English it means "place
of love or home". O books explores the many paths of
understanding which different traditions have developed
down the ages, particularly those today that express
respect for the planet and all of life.

For more information on the full list of over 300 titles
please visit our website
**www.O-books.net**

# SOME RECENT O BOOKS

## Good As New
John Henson

*A short review cannot begin to persuade readers of the value of this book. If you feel you can really face what Jesus and the writers of the New Testament really meant rather than have your ears dulled by the versions we normally hear, then buy this book-and read it. But only if you are brave enough.* **Renew**
1905047118 448pp £11.99 $19.95


## Who on EARTH was JESUS?
**the modern quest for the Jesus of history**
David Boulton

*What happens when the Christ of faith meets the Jesus of history? This is the question that preoccupies Boulton in an amazingly good synthesis of historical Jesus scholarship. His scope is as wide-ranging as it is even-handed; from theologians to scholars to popes, he distills their thoughts into a comprehensible and comprehensive survey of the best of the contemporary thinkers. Readers will find no overt proselytizing in this book. Instead, the author treats them to an unbiased look at the ever-changing discipline of Jesus studies. In the end, Boulton understands that it is not the scholar, nor the theologian, who will define the kingdom on Earth. Rather, it will be the job of all of us to discern the Jesus of today from words written long ago. This book is not to be missed.* **Publisher's Weekly**
9781846940187 448pp £14.99 $29.95

# Bringing God Back to Earth
John Hunt

*Knowledgeable in theology, philosophy, science and history. Time and again it is remarkable how he brings the important issues into relation with one another... thought provoking in almost every sentence, difficult to put down.* **Faith and Freedom**
1903816815 320pp £9.99 $14.95

# Gospel of Falling Down
**The beauty of failure, in an age of success**
Mark Townsend

*It's amazing just how far I was drawn into Mark's words. This wasn't just a book but an experience. I never realized that failure could be a creative process.* **Editor,** 'Voila' Magazine
1846940095 144pp £9.99 $16.95

# Liberal Faith in a Divided Church
Jonathan Clatworthy

*This is a truly radical book, in that it looks for the roots of a liberal approach to Christianity that is principled, inclusive and undogmatic. Jonathan Clatworthy shows how liberal faith has always striven to temper the wisdom of the past with the promptings of the Spirit in the present. Rather than seeing such an approach as a departure from true orthodoxy, he demonstrates that they lie at the heart of a consistent vision of God's relationship with the world. This book will provide encouragement and sustenance for those who wish for an alternative to absolute certainty, in its secular and religious forms.* **Elaine Graham,** Professor of Social and Pastoral Theology, University of Manchester
9781846941160 272pp £14.99 $29.95